M000093116

DISCIPLINE WIN

ANDY JACKS

DISCIPLINE
WIN

STRATEGIES TO
IMPROVE BEHAVIOR,
INCREASE OWNERSHIP, AND
GIVE EVERY STUDENT A CHANCE

Discipline Win: Strategies to Improve Behavior, Increase Ownership, and Give Every Student a Chance
© 2021 Andy Jacks

All rights reserved. No part of this publication may be reproduced in any form or by any electronic or mechanical means, including information storage and retrieval systems, without permission in writing by the publisher, except by a reviewer who may quote brief passages in a review. For information regarding permission, contact the publisher at books@daveburgessconsulting.com.

This book is available at special discounts when purchased in quantity for use for educational purposes or as premiums, promotions, or fundraisers. For inquiries and details, contact the publisher at books@daveburgessconsulting.com.

Published by Dave Burgess Consulting, Inc. San Diego, CA

DaveBurgessConsulting.com

Library of Congress Control Number: 2021943978

Paperback ISBN: 978-1-951600-97-6

Ebook ISBN: 978-1-951600-98-3

Cover and interior design by Liz Schreiter

Editing and production by Reading List Editorial: readinglisteditorial.com

This book is dedicated to the heroes in the classroom
that are doing the real work every day.

To the students that feel like they are different
or don't belong.

To all those who never gave up on me and instead
gave me the extra chances I didn't deserve.

And to my family for their love and patience and for
always having my back.

CONTENTS

FOREWORD

BY HAMISH BREWER

THE RELENTLESS, TATTOOED, SKATEBOARDING PRINCIPAL

I want us to all remember why we signed up to be educators, what it felt like that very first day we walked into a school or met the very first class or group of students we had. Never forget that feeling, that vision, and that dream.

In education today—almost to a fault sometimes—we will shout to the mountain tops how we want all kids to succeed, all schools to be equitable, and all kids to be offered every opportunity to grow and shine. But the difference between rhetoric and action—between perceptions and the realities of systems, processes, and policies—can often be incredible. Especially when it comes to discipline in schools, it can seem like everyone is an expert. It's easy to come up with a great gimmick or plan for how you're going to help improve student discipline and outcomes. However, the reality is that many of these ideas are often overcomplicated and focus on containment and management—helping educators and kids survive school, not thrive in it.

It's time to stop overthinking the work we do as educators. In *Discipline Win*, Dr. Andy Jacks shows us that often the best solution is the simplest. Andy is challenging you, as he has challenged me over the years, with a call to action to reflect both personally and professionally about how you perceive and believe in our students. That's the first step to rethinking how our schools really and truly can accept and love all students unconditionally.

I have been fortunate to observe and watch Andy in action for years. It's hard not to be biased when talking about the work of one of your best friends, but a true friend holds you accountable, challenges you, celebrates you, lifts you up, and is there for you in both the good and bad times. Andy has consistently pushed not only his own expectations for success but those of everyone around him, willing them to want to work harder, think deeper, and go further than they ever thought they could. It is not uncommon for Andy to challenge his leaders and educators to truly drill down and understand that the last 10 percent is just as important as the first 10 percent—to go after every single child, leaving no one behind. To this end, Andy has ensured that right alongside high standards for engagement and relationships, high academic results are achieved. And year after year, Andy has to his credit some of the highest academic results across all content areas, banging on the door of 100 percent pass rates and smashing state-exam expectations. Real work, real results. Difference makers like Andy don't just talk about the work, they roll their sleeves up and do it. They not only want to make a profound impact on pastoral care, engagement, and children's well-being, but they see opportunities for academic success.

Andy and I have had long, deep, and hard conversations about how to best protect, nurture, and care for students. As colleagues, we've held each other to the expectation that there is absolutely no excuse to suspend a student, that there is always another way, and we should always look for other solutions. Easier said than done—and tough to stand by when it can seem that many stakeholders could care less or believe in a lower standard or an easier solution—but Andy's results have now shown beyond a doubt that the way we have traditionally approached school and student discipline does not always work and that it doesn't have to be the way things are done.

Unfortunately, it can seem that not much has changed. We have all too often fallen back on the idea that tougher is better, harder is better, zero tolerance is better. In fact, without the integration of root-cause analyses and scaffolded support and structures, "tough" responses often reinforce the very thing we are trying to abate. Instead of a reactive, archaic discipline process centered around "gotchas," we should engage in proactive processes that focus on how we can help students by reimagining our opportunities with our stakeholders.

Andy has a saying: "Your school is defined by how you treat your most at-risk students." It's easy when all your students come to school equipped and ready to succeed, but when we start to work with real trauma, academic failure, mental-health concerns, and the well-being of our students, we truly begin to find out who we are, how far we are willing to go, and how we respond under stress.

I believe that children struggling with behavior at school are children crying out for help and connection. In many cases behavior issues are a manifestation of not just issues with home environments but—just as importantly, I believe—with the acquisition of basic skills such as the ability to read, write, and compute simple math. As children progress through increasingly difficult curricula and grades, skill gaps become greater and, without intervention, the stakes rise in terms of engagement, participation, and success, both academically and emotionally. Our students are struggling with issues around mental health and well-being more than ever before. Youth suicide is at a high in so many places around the world. Students are feeling isolated and withdrawing into their own silent worlds. Who can they reach out and connect to? Who will stand up and fight for them? Fundamentally, these children are waiting for an opportunity to let us in to help; if we don't, the ultimate outcome can potentially be that our schools become pipelines to prison. That's something we cannot allow or tolerate.

Discipline Win helps you really reimagine your relationships with students and the possibilities for each stakeholder in schools from the ground up. It challenges us to look beyond a single action or outcome and into the root causes and structures that create the how and why of the challenges in schools. Only once we better understand and love our students can we truly help them make their own strides toward their best selves.

THE MEANING BEHIND DISCIPLINE WIN

"We *will* get her to walk."

Dr. Rachel Alachnowicz, our school's physical therapist, wasn't messing around. I could see a glint of rebelliousness in her eye as she said these words. She was talking about one of our students who was affected by serious physical difficulties. Since this little girl was at an early age, her parents had been told that she would be physically and mentally disabled so much that it would prevent her from being able to walk independently during her lifetime. Her mom told me how the doctor used the word "never" when explaining this to her. *Never*. When she came to school to learn, she required the use of a wheelchair and a lot of assistance from adults.

"We *will* get her to walk."

Rachel was on a mission to have this little girl be able to walk and function at a higher level, and she went all in to make it happen: She took extra time to add padded walking and moving areas in the classroom. And she challenged the staff—practically yelling at them to get the student up and moving and out of her seat. New strategies were implemented and practiced every single day. Soon, the girl started to walk with a walker. Then holding on to an adult. Finally, people started to see that the impossible goal wasn't actually impossible at all. Better yet, they started to *believe*.

Then, one day, word spread around school that the little girl was in the hallway walking on her own. I came rushing down to see for myself, literally dropping everything I was doing at the time. Seeing some of her first steps will forever be engrained in my memories. She was determined and yet gleeful as this new part of her life opened up to her. She was doing it all on her own, slowly making her claim on life one step at a time down the hallway.

Later, after calling the girl's mother to share the good news and celebrate together on the phone, I sat and reflected in silence at how much of a miracle this was for this family. All because of the will and desire of our teachers to push forward and not listen to what others were saying about their students' "limitations." Rachel and the team took that "limit" as a challenge and absolutely destroyed it. Like so many of our teachers out there finding ways to push past barriers in their students' way, Rachel was able to trust her gut and literally inspire a miracle for her student. There is only one "never" we should think about: we must *never* accept limitations for success that others put on our students.

Besides those first steps, what I remember most about this situation is more about Rachel's attitude than her actions. In fact, I really don't recall the specific strategies that were used, although I know how important they were. When I think of that time, I can still remember the passion that engulfed Rachel like a powerful aura. I could feel it when she walked by me. There is nothing quite like witnessing the pride teachers have in their students achieving "impossible" goals.

Nothing is truly impossible, if the mindset of those responding to the crisis is this focused. Rachel and the rest of the team changed that girl's and her family's lives forever. Their dedication and leadership made the difference. It inspired the rest of the team working with this child to also challenge that status quo, which ultimately affected so many students following in literally the same footsteps and needing the same push for improvement.

WHAT IS DISCIPLINE?

You may be reading this and saying aloud, "But Andy, I thought I was reading a book about school discipline!"

My response? Absolutely. Yes! But it also depends on how you view discipline.

There are so many opinions on how we should discipline our kids that it can be overwhelming to know how to even think about this topic. The Merriam-Webster dictionary describes discipline as "a hardship imposed in response to a crime or offense" and lists synonyms such as "punishment, wrath, revenge, and imprisonment." This mirrors the traditional zero-tolerance approach that many of us grew up with and consider normal.

It took me a long time, but after a lot of experience and research, I realized how wrong this view of discipline we often see in schools really is. We associate "disciplining" our students with control, power, and compliance, but as we think of "discipline" in our own lives as adults, we hope for more uplifting words like motivation, habits, and grace.

It helps to consider how we would want to be treated as adults. The Golden Rule—to treat others as you would want to be treated—never gets old. That's how we should be treating discipline with our students, to help them refocus their actions, habits, and decisions to be more aligned with the goals they have for their future.

It helps to view this through historical context such as in the Latin word *disciplina,* meaning teaching, learning, and growing, or the French word *disciple,* meaning the practice of training to obey rules or code of conduct.

It helps to realize where your personal philosophy on discipline comes from. There are many ways to view discipline, but my major goal is for you to take ownership of your personal philosophy on discipline and how it will drive your decisions on what to do when things get tough with your students. So much of school discipline starts with *our* self-discipline.

GETTING CALLED OUT

No matter how great we are as teachers and leaders, there are moments in your life that reset your entire world view on the work we do with kids.

One of those moments was when a parent called me out. It changed me. We were standing in my office at the time, and I had just informed her we were going to suspend her child. She was obviously upset. She looked me straight in the eyes, peering deep into my soul, and said with a quiet but fierce passion, "Dr. Jacks, you say you are about all kids and will do whatever it takes, but I have my child right in front of you asking for help. And now you are going to kick him to the curb. What are you going to do for my child if you're about all kids?"

Wow! That was a real moment and a gut punch. She was absolutely right. It was my call as principal. It ultimately was my decision. I had the authority to go in many directions, and at the time I picked the more convenient option for the school, not the best one for that child.

Ever since that moment, I've fought back on every instance of exclusion and suspension. If a child was going to be removed from our school, it would have to go through me first. I would own each and every decision and weigh it against what was best for that individual child. If I'm about ALL kids, then I have to be about the ones that get in trouble and are hard to reach, too. It's reminded me about my why—my purpose—and has given me a new drive in what I do as an educator. Sometimes we need others to call us out like this!

WHAT IS WINNING?

NFL coach Herm Edwards once stated very emphatically, "You play to win the game." That's exactly the mentality we need with discipline. We're not just coming to work. We're playing to win. Every day. Every situation. Every student. And just because we may get knocked back on some plays or lose some of the games, doesn't mean that we give up or stop trying. We play to win the game. If we want a discipline win, then we need to know how to play the game, what plays are the most effective at reaching our goals, and better yet, how to help our players on the field—the students—to practice with conviction and a championship mentality.

I wrote this book with educators in mind, adding ideas and suggestions that would actually make a difference so that teachers could turn their situations around. Why? The call to action from parents and even from students gave me the drive for change, but the teachers I worked with gave me the direction. I remember too many times working through difficult moments with my teachers and not having a real answer for them on what to do next. Teachers deserve more than just platitudes and positive attitudes. They deserve solutions. For me that meant I had to get better. I had to learn. This led me on a journey of discovery: reading everything I could get my hands on, focusing on discipline for my doctoral dissertation, forming discipline committees and focus groups, and ultimately doing the research for this book.

Winning in discipline isn't really about misconduct or what to do when kids misbehave. The misbehavior we observe is a by-product of deeper issues in education and society. It's often due to factors outside the student's control. *Discipline Win* presents a proactive approach, helping our kids stay in school, be engaged in the process of self-development, and feel like they belong to the group. It's about inclusion and how to inspire a new culture of acceptance in our schools and classrooms with the results being that our schools look different based on the students we serve and are more responsive to the needs they have and the desires in learning that they express.

Discipline should not be what we do to kids. Discipline should be what we do for kids. Effective discipline should plan on teaching students new skills on how to work with others, how to regulate their emotions and behaviors, and how to align their actions with their goals in life. It goes back to the basics, helping kids learn to do the right thing—because it's the right thing, not because it's the rule. This idea is not mine alone; it's based on the latest advice in modern child—and adult—psychology.

PRACTICAL AND PHILOSOPHICAL SUGGESTIONS FOR IMPROVEMENT

No individual book will cover everything on a topic, and there are many great books on discipline. Read them all. *Discipline Win* is my take on a really tough topic, meant to be both practical and philosophical in nature since both are necessary to rethink this topic. Each chapter shares a lesson that we can use to grow both ourselves and our students. Included are takeaways and activities you can use in your classroom and school right now:

CHAPTER 1: Welcome every child as a gift to your classroom. Understand and want them as a whole child, even with the challenges they bring with them to school.

CHAPTER 2: Have an intense sense of urgency, acting in ways to prevent your students from failing. Embrace the idea that educators are also first responders.

CHAPTER 3: Don't default to archaic principals of punishment and shame. Instead use what works: processes and systems to slow down, investigate, and rethink our reactions to misconduct.

CHAPTER 4: Allow students to own their own growth and paths for improvement. See every child as a leader that can have a great influence on themselves and their peers.

CHAPTER 5: Dig deeper into situations to learn about context and root causes so that the plans you make actually address the real issues.

CHAPTER 6: Strategically and purposefully teach students how to behave. Instructions for discipline should be clear and taught just like any other academic subject.

CHAPTER 7: Capitalize on growing relationships to make improvements. Learn how social-cognitive learning is key to helping students understand how to improve behaviors.

CHAPTER 8: Show students how to develop their own skills in self-regulation and discipline. Real strategies and tools are needed, not just talking about feelings.

CHAPTER 9: Focus on supporting and involving families in the process. Realize how much we can do to work with families instead of against them.

CHAPTER 10: Ensure fidelity and follow-through in interventions to ensure long-term success. Consider how your dedication to the process influences the results as much as the intervention itself.

At the end of each chapter is a "Time-Out" to give a moment of reflection for that chapter's lesson. I purposely chose "time-out" as a heading for its double meaning. It's a perfect reminder of how education can take a positive term and twist it negatively. Time-outs in sports are helpful. They give players a rest. They give an opportunity to draw up a game-winning play. They bring players and coaches together. No one ever thinks players are in trouble if the coach calls time-out.

But time-outs in discipline become dark quickly. They become punishment and exclusion, when they really could be more positive and growth-producing like in sports. It's time we take these terms back!

I hope to share strategies that may help you and advice based on the many achievements I have had with all types of students, but *Discipline Win* isn't about me telling you how perfect I am with discipline. Far from it. I've done a lot of great work, but I've struggled so many times. I've felt the pain of both physical violence from students and the heartbreak of failure from not being able to really help them. In fact, so much of what drove me to do more reading, research, and self-reflection came from my feelings of inadequacy as a leader and educator. I hope that sharing stories of these struggles can show that we are not alone in this work. Many lessons were learned the hard way, through mistakes and shortcomings. Taught to me by my colleagues and staff. By my students and their parents. By my own teachers growing up. The lessons shared in this book are a tribute to the selfless acts of heroism by teachers that I have been fortunate enough to witness over the years. What it comes down to is this: If we want to have different results, we have to do different actions and be different in our entire approach. Even the best can rethink how they do things, and ultimately I'm just asking you to do that. Reconsider your approach. Check your actions. Own your decisions.

My process of reflection and vulnerability created a new excitement and passion for kids that I can honestly say I didn't have before. I hope to share with you the journey that has led me to a philosophy that is now the core of my being and so much more than just discipline. I am here for my kids. No matter what. For whatever they need and whenever they need it. If you want to take a child out of my building, you are coming through me first. I will do everything I possibly can to help a child succeed, even when it's extremely difficult. Usually the harder it gets, the more I know I'm in the right place and at the right time because how we support our most struggling kids is really what defines us as educators and schools.

I know there are so many educators that feel beat up right now. That feel like their situation is unfair and that educators are so often blamed for things they can't control. I've been there, feeling beat up both physically and emotionally. But as Sylvester Stallone said so well, "Nobody is gonna hit as hard as life, but it ain't how hard you can hit. It's how hard you can get hit and keep moving forward. It's how much you can take and keep moving forward. That's how winning is done."

You are stronger than your situation. You too can own every choice you make, acting and reacting in ways that not only get you back up off the mat, but also inspire great changes in others around you. It's a special feeling to realize that when we accept the work for what it is, we can find peace in the very difficult tasks ahead and learn how to even find joy in them. These challenges we face end up changing us in ways we could never even predict. That's why we should thank these kids for bringing us these challenges: they make us better educators.

Rachel challenged us to move from "this child can't walk" to "this child will walk and I'm going to show her how!" We then can move from "students won't behave" to "students will behave and we're going to show them how!" We can do this! Let's run into these situations with the same sense of purpose, the same sense of urgency, and the same determination to make the real difference we all know drove us into teaching in the first place!

CHAPTER 1

UNDERSTAND, WELCOME, AND WANT EVERY CHILD

IT IS NOT OUR DIFFERENCES THAT DIVIDE US. IT IS OUR INABILITY TO RECOGNIZE, ACCEPT, AND CELEBRATE THOSE DIFFERENCES. —AUDRE LORDE

When I first started teaching, I was hired to teach fifth grade in a small, low-income, diverse Title I school. I excitedly set up my classroom, organized my materials, and rearranged my desks about ten times before I had them just the way I wanted them. I wanted to change the world and be a great teacher, but I have to admit I had butterflies in my stomach as I anticipated standing in front of my first students.

As I was double-checking my preparations, thinking I was all set to go, I saw the principal walking a mother and daughter my way down the hall. Meeting me at the door to the classroom, the child smiled and said, "Hola."

Whoa.

I replied, "Uh . . . hola," as I realized that neither the little girl nor her mother spoke any English. I knew practically no Spanish and had little more than a smile to offer her in that moment. My butterflies turned into a near panic attack as I realized how unprepared I was for my students coming into class that day.

Then the school bell rang. The day was just getting started, and I was already overwhelmed.

Welcome to teaching.

I knew my students would bring all sorts of personalities, backgrounds, and experiences to the class. But I had given no thought whatsoever to needing to be prepared in *this* way. But let me be clear: it was my fault, not the student's. She had done absolutely nothing wrong. She had simply come to school ready to learn and be accepted. She was assuming that her teacher would be prepared to work with her.

I should have been more prepared.

PAST "TYPICAL" STUDENTS AND "TYPICAL" SCHOOLS

We teach over fifty-five million students in our American public and private schools today. What's more impressive is that our schools are now more inclusive than ever. More students with disabilities, students of color, students for whom English is not a first language, and students with trauma are taught alongside their peers than before. A few generations ago, many of these students would not be in our public schools. They would be home, in institutions, or otherwise shut out of the school system altogether for so many different reasons.

Because of the increased inclusion of all students, we need to rethink what typically is needed in schools. It's not always effective to simply deal with an urgent situation so that you can move on with your class to get back to "normal," whatever that is. Ideas of what is "normal" in schools based on older systems that would have excluded many of the students we have the privilege of working with today simply don't apply. It's critical to know your students, what makes each one special, and the needs they have in and out of school.

UNDERSTANDING AND ACCEPTING

Over the years, I have spent so much time hand in hand with families that had children with disabilities. Many of you may have a child or a loved one with a disability yourself. I do in my family. These experiences have changed me, as they should, especially regarding inclusion.

Inclusion is not just about "awareness." That's too easy and too simplistic. Your students don't need to just be seen, as if that will fix everything. Awareness alone implies that other students and staff have more power or more value and that they have the power to grant those rights and feelings to others. All our kids already have those rights, whether they realize it or not.

Our entire school culture should revolve around welcoming and wanting every student, no matter what they look like, their abilities, or how much money their family makes. But before we start working on students' social skills, let's first talk about the adults in the room. It starts with us. Our words, actions, and reactions all demonstrate how we value, accept, and support our students. And like in most things, actions are the real evidence of your intent. Kids can always tell if you really do accept them for who they are or not, and your positive words of kindness won't mean a thing if your actions and emotions show something different.

The first step is to understand who the students are that you serve and what they may need. Instead of blaming them or their parents for their shortcomings, we need to understand and accept them for who they are, not who we expected them to be. I think in many ways teachers are set up from the beginning. We are given this idealistic version of school that is just not reality. It becomes a shock to the system when things get real and get real fast. We need to help new teachers especially by preparing them with the skills to be as prepared for the outliers as the teacher's pet.

So let's look at two large groups of students that are typically on the low end of the behavioral bell curve: students with disabilities and students who are dealing with trauma.

Students with Disabilities

Students with disabilities include school-age students who are serviced under the Individuals with Disabilities Education Act (IDEA). IDEA guarantees these students specific rights, such as a Free Appropriate Public Education and an individualized education program (IEP).

In the educational landscape, we are continuing to see an increase over time regarding the amount and percentage of students that are serviced through special education. It will help to know what disabilities to expect in the classroom.

Students with disabilities are not just a few students in the corner of the room. According to the National Center for Education Statistics, now 14 percent of all students are considered disabled, almost double from when IDEA was implemented in 1976. Of these students, nearly two-thirds of them are male.

Specific learning disability (SLD) is by far the most common disability among disabled students, with 33 percent of disabled students having SLD.[1] Students with SLD have disorders in processing and understanding language, reading, and/mathematical calculations. Students with processing disorders, such as dyslexia, may struggle with behavior due to lack of academic progress or feelings of low self-esteem.

Autism spectrum disorder now accounts for 11 percent of all disabled students, up from less than 2 percent in the early 2000s. As with so many other disorders we are discussing here, this is not something

---

1 National Center for Education Statistics, "Fast Facts: Students with Disabilities," nces.ed.gov/fastfacts/display.asp?id=64.

easily figured out through a blood test. Doctors use behavioral assessments to look for trends in behaviors that are typical to this disability. Autistic students exhibit a broad range of conditions characterized by challenges with social skills, repetitive behaviors, speech and nonverbal communication, and executive functioning.

These disabilities and disorders do not mean that these kids will necessarily be unintelligent or misbehave or both. Students with autism for example, can have very high IQs but behaviorally struggle due to sensory issues or disconnects in executive functioning.

According to the Centers for Disease and Control, almost 10 percent of all students are identified as having attention-deficit/hyperactivity disorder (ADHD).[2] ADHD presents in many ways in our students, such as difficulty paying attention, problems controlling impulsive behaviors, or being overly active. Boys are twice as likely to be diagnosed with ADHD than girls.

Six percent of students are diagnosed with a behavior disorder, which includes oppositional defiance disorder (ODD) and conduct disorder (CD). That means that we should expect at least 6 percent of our students to exhibit frequent and persistent patterns of anger, irritability, arguing, defiance, or vindictiveness toward authority. Severity, duration, and the effect on school and family identify this as a disorder rather than common misbehavior.

A growing percentage of students are being diagnosed with anxiety and/or depression. Typically it has been adults that have been diagnosed with anxiety, but for a variety of reasons, we are now seeing it more in our school-age children. Especially in higher income schools, this increasing number of students with anxiety is being seen as a new norm in our classrooms.

Consider even students identified as gifted. This is an area often overlooked because of how "successful" many of these students are academically. Gifted students display many strengths in performance and learning, but they also have certain tendencies that sometimes

2 Centers for Disease Control and Prevention, "Data and Statistics on Children's Mental Health," March 22, 2021, cdc.gov/childrensmentalhealth/data.html.

interfere with their own or other's learning, such as rigidity in expectations, need for control of their environment, cynical predictions, social difficulties, and perfectionism.

Finally, the conversation about students with disabilities must include the significant and disproportional number of students of color being labeled as disabled. Students of color, particularly Black students, are identified for special education at a much higher rate than their white peers. For instance, Black students are 40 percent more likely to be identified as disabled than all other students. Many other books and articles do a great job of breaking this down, with reasons why these rates occur and the harm it causes our students.

The answer to support for students with disabilities is typically an individualized education program, but be careful how much we advocate for this plan and then feel like the plan alone will fix everything. Knowing kids have different abilities is one thing, but as we will discuss more, the real trick is doing something about it with fidelity and follow-through over a long time.

Students Who Have Experienced Trauma

The highest percentage of students with a behavioral disorder that we see in our schools are those dealing with some type of trauma. According to the National Child Traumatic Stress Network, two-thirds of our students will have experienced a traumatic event by age sixteen.[3] With schools dealing with the effect of a pandemic, the idea of our students having trauma is not a new concept to many of you.

Trauma, or adverse childhood experiences (ACES) occurs in many ways but can cause behavior outwardly mimicking that seen in other behavioral disorders, including poor self-regulation, negative self-talk, hypervigilance on fairness, lack of concentration, difficulty sleeping, self-harming behaviors, eating disorders, and trouble forming relationships, especially with adults.

---

3 National Child Traumatic Stress Network, "Trauma-Informed Schools for Children in K–12: A System Framework," nctsn.org/sites/default/files/resources/fact-sheet/trauma_informed_ schools_for_children_in_k-12_a_systems_framework.pdf.

Supporting students that have experienced significant trauma can be daunting. We all need a lot more professional learning in this area. Schools *absolutely* need trained psychologists and counselors to address the root of these issues. We need more counselors. We need more psychologists and social workers. Teachers can't do this work on their own. We need experts doing expert work!

In the meantime, consider a few basic strategies we can do now in our schools that can help. These may seem obvious and simplistic, and on a surface level they may be, but I assure you they are not easy to do consistently well.

Be positive: Students need your patience and love especially when they express challenging behaviors. As caring adults, we need to be unconditionally positive in our responses, showing that we care about them and modeling the appropriate behaviors we wish to see in return.

Be predictable: Students feel safer when they can predict their day and your actions, so use routines and consistency in your classroom as well as staying consistent in your personal mood. Keep expectations high and maintain those for all students.

Be inquisitive: Some students won't share with you unless you ask them, so set aside time for them to do this. Be careful not to make assumptions and instead talk with them, actively listening and being present so you can learn more about what they are going through.

Be responsive: Students trust you more when you regularly and consistently respond to their needs and their requests. Trust builds based on your follow-through.

There are many more ways to understand your students: race, religion, gender identity—the list goes on and on. These other aspects are not disabilities, but they do create a better understanding for the diverse group of students that you may or may not be used to interacting with in your personal life. It's understandable if differences may make you initially uncomfortable, but that better stop right there and not continue long term. When we accept the role of a professional educator, we better remember the word professional in the title. Being professional means that we think more about the work than our personal viewpoints or bias. Regardless of your personal beliefs, our job as educators is to make sure students feel that we are accepting them for who they are and welcome them with open arms. Not asking them to be different or change, but just as they are.

BE CAREFUL NOT TO COMPARE

Our classrooms are complex because we have students with so many different levels and needs. Something I consider a major hidden issue in schools is the effect of age on grade-level expectations. Malcolm Gladwell, in his book *Outliers: The Story of Success*, describes the effects of birthdates and timing for cut-off dates in sports and academic success. Gladwell claims that students that are older and more mature have more skills than their peers and thus outperform them. Because they perform better, they make better connections with their teachers and coaches. In turn, they receive more praise, attention, and extra teaching. They gain favor and end up getting more opportunities. The extra attention has a further effect of pushing them even further ahead.

Since students are literally all at different ages, even within the same grade level, and they develop at different rates, we need to be very careful comparing the ways they act learn. We often praise students at the upper levels of learning and success in schools, but often those successes are due to development and environments that they had no control over. They might have been lucky to land in a family with plentiful resources, support, and love. Or they might have a brain that developed at a faster rate. Both are outside of their control, yet they receive disproportionate praise, as if their successes were due solely to their hard work.

On the other end, we have students that struggle for so many different reasons, such as due to a disability, trauma, or a lack of resources or positive experiences at home, but we expect them to develop skills at the same rate as others. When they don't, they are often shamed, blamed, or punished for these aspects of their lives that are outside their control.

RESPONSE TO INTERVENTION, MULTI-TIERED SYSTEMS OF SUPPORT, AND BELL CURVES

Response to intervention (RTI) emerged years ago as a way to identify students who are struggling and help schools align interventions and supports according to different tiers of needs and is often represented in a pyramid-shaped diagram, broken down into three tiers. Tier 1 consists of most of the students and focuses on "first instruction" to achieve a mastery level of the learning objectives. If mastery or other adequate performance is not attained, additional supports and services are provided based on student-performance data for some students at tier 2 and only a few at tier 3.

RTI is an effective model because it reminds us that we need to *proactively* have things set up and in place for *all* students, knowing that the first instruction will not work for all kids. While many use RTI for academics, using it to identify different tiers of behavior is a great way to plan for the intensity and frequency of support for your students.

TIER 1 includes general instruction on how to behave. Teachers help students understand the rules and expectations through teaching and practice. Behaviors that arise are organically addressed through redirection and reteaching. Classroom-management systems are created to provide positive rewards and motivators. Daily work on interpersonal skills and collaboration is emphasized. Practices are research- or evidence-based. Reteaching for small groups and individuals addresses repeated errors in class.

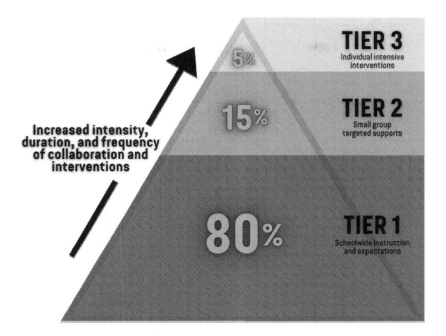

TIER 3
Individual intensive interventions

TIER 2
Small group targeted supports

TIER 1
Schoolwide instruction and expectations

5%

15%

80%

Increased intensity, duration, and frequency of collaboration and interventions

TIER 2 includes additional instruction for students who need it based on their misconduct in class and school. Instruction includes targeted interventions for individuals or small groups based on specific areas of need. Progress is monitored and instruction adjusted. The goal is for students to make sufficient progress to not need this level of support in the future.

TIER 3 includes intensive levels of intervention. Lessons are individualized with a narrow focus based on the most interfering behaviors. More time is spent away from class to provide this level of support. Family services and community resources are provided.

Over time, RTI evolved into a new perspective and model of the same concept, called Multi-Tiered Systems of Support (MTSS). MTSS is a whole-child approach that includes behavior and social-emotional learning and enables schools to strategically consider students' behaviors using data, just as they would academic performance.

You may be reading this thinking that this is old news or common sense, and on the surface, it may be, but when we dig in to it, some questions emerge.

One of the ongoing questions that schools have with RTI or MTSS is how to include students with disabilities in the tiered organization scheme. Are they in tier 3, a separate tier 4, or are they even included in this diagram? It drove me crazy at first to see students that needed the most help appear to be excluded from this model. Here's a quick tip: If your most struggling students are not even included in your intervention model, then you are not an inclusive school.

IF YOUR MOST STRUGGLING STUDENTS ARE NOT EVEN INCLUDED IN YOUR INTERVENTION MODEL, THEN YOU ARE NOT AN INCLUSIVE SCHOOL.

Also consider this: RTI is referenced in the Individuals with Disabilities Education Act (IDEA) in 2004 as a way to *ensure* that students are not inappropriately identified as disabled. That was a head-scratcher for us when we worked through this. Were we doing this? Were we *ensuring* that students were provided support and reteaching before they totally failed? Were we using *systems* to identify students in need and then monitor their progress?

As a school, we bought into RTI and then MTSS, more so with the philosophy than any one specific intervention. We completely changed how we included not only special education students, but all students we served, by turning the pyramid model on its head, or in this case, its side. Educators are amazingly rebellious. For a group that teaches kids how to follow directions, educators are notorious for redefining norms and challenging the status quo. That's exactly what happened in our school with leaders like our Reading Specialist, Crystal Watt, and many others that reframed our thinking of what a real system of support looks like in a real school with real issues.

Along with a few others I found thinking the same thing, we shoved with all our might and tipped the pyramid over on its side. We added another pyramid in reverse on the other side. We transformed it into a diamond. The middle section is now tier 1 and the left side has a tier 2 and tier 3 for "below expected performance" like we see in a typical MTSS pyramid. The right side is new and represents the other end of the extreme, with additional tiers 2 and 3 for "above expected performance."

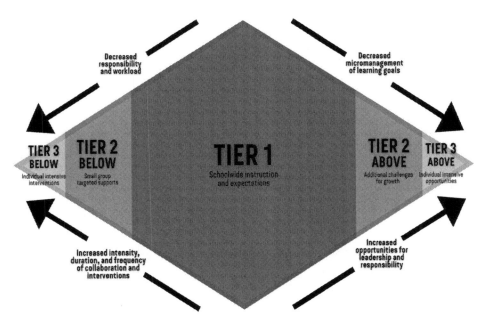

The diamond model was a more accurate depiction of our student body as a whole. Our students are not just good or bad, positive or negative, well behaved or misbehaved. They are complex and diverse. Instead of focusing only on students who misbehave, the diamond model reminded us that we also have students that go above and beyond to be kind, to be helpful, and to be positive leaders. When we acknowledged this, we realized the many positive aspects of every single classroom. There are no "bad" classes. Every class is a mix of ability levels that deserves to be viewed with facts instead of emotions, especially when it comes to behaviors.

We immediately began new interventions with a sense of urgency. If a student needs help today, they will receive support tomorrow if not sooner. That automaticity is a cultural norm that is both effective and powerful in helping the mindset change on how we are ready for kids that will inevitably need more help.

Another way to reframe this is to compare it to a bell curve. A bell curve represents a normal distribution of scores, which in this case, we are basing on student behavioral performance. The highest point of the curve shows the most common performance from our students, and each end of the left and right includes fewer students whose behavior is less common.

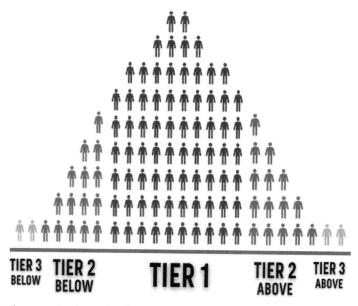

When we look at the diamond or bell curve models, it's incredibly important to note one thing: Students don't *become* tier 2 or tier 3. They are already there. It's our job to provide the supports they need based on those levels.

It's also important to remember that we *can* affect outcomes for our students and the dynamics of their whole classes. Students behave differently with different teachers. For classrooms that are run poorly and not managed with effective and proactive discipline, the curve will appear to be skewed toward misconduct. Students in those classes then appear to be set up for failure and may be labeled as part of the "bad" class. This can become part of a self-fulfilling prophecy, with staff unintentionally treating them according to a label they received due to a teacher's effectiveness.

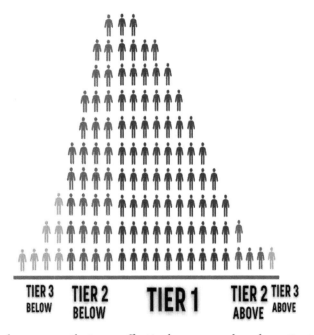

| TIER 3 BELOW | TIER 2 BELOW | TIER 1 | TIER 2 ABOVE | TIER 3 ABOVE |

For classrooms that are effectively managed and motivated, with extra behavioral instruction and focus, the curve skews in a positive direction, and students might be labeled as part of a "good" class. Yes, we do have different abilities, but it's critical to understand that each group is made up of individuals.

TIER 2 BELOW **TIER 1** **TIER 2 ABOVE** **TIER 3 ABOVE**

Think of the amazing power we have to skew the entire curve. The best educators go into each year determined to completely change the trajectory of the class coming their way, like, "This is my world, kids, and get ready to live in it and be successful, whether you like it not!" Even kids that come in grumbling will begin to buy in once they see how right you were!

There are no "bad" classes or "good" classes. Every class, just like every student, is unique and special. Educators that find joy in the differences, quirkiness, or even challenge are the ones that will be the most successful. Be curious and find something that fascinates you about every child. You can't fake it. Not to yourself or to the kids in front of you.

Try this strategy to rethink your class. Create a bell curve using your current students and a criterion like work completion, participation, general respect and obedience, or collaboration. Draw the curve or diamond shape on a large piece of paper. Then write each of your students' names on a sticky note, and place them in each section: well above, above, average, below, well below. Use data as much as you can for these decisions. At the elementary level, this can be done with your homeroom class you may have most of the day. For other types of teachers that see many classes in a day or teachers at the secondary level, you may want to pick your most challenging class or even do this one class at a time.

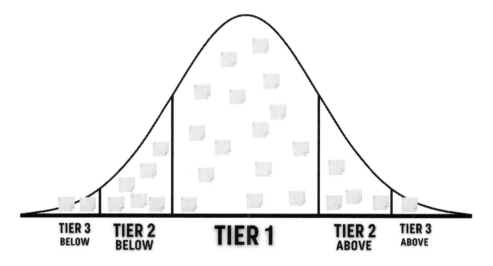

| TIER 3 | TIER 2 | TIER 1 | TIER 2 | TIER 3 |
| BELOW | BELOW | | ABOVE | ABOVE |

Break down the percentages of students in each tier. Identify any trends that come up to check any potential bias with race or gender. Share and compare your class with a colleague. Do you have drastically different amounts of students in each performance level? If so, why?

Did you make the decisions on placement of students in each tier based on data or based on your feelings in the moment? If you don't have a lot of information to help you make decisions more objectively, that also tells you something: you need more behavioral checks for progress or performance.

Once you have looked at the trends overall, take additional time to consider what your current reality is with behaviors and instruction to help determine any additional gaps or next steps for improvement. You can do this by taking those sticky notes or even just writing the names into a new chart like the one that follows.

TIERS	TIER 3 BELOW	TIER 2 BELOW	TIER 1	TIER 2 ABOVE	TIER 3 ABOVE
STUDENTS					
CURRENT REALITY					
CURRENT INSTRUCTION & SUPPORTS					
NEXT STEPS FOR IMPROVEMENT					

Reflect, discuss, and write down notes about the current realities for behavior in your classroom for each of these groups. What are they doing well? What behaviors are interfering with instruction and their learning?

List the current instruction and supports you are providing for students in each of these levels. Do not overlook basic teaching and reteaching you do with all kids as unimportant. During this process, you may find gaps in your current instruction and supports for students that are struggling behaviorally.

With colleagues, brainstorm ways to reteach or intervene so that students can make progress in areas where they struggle. So often, the answer is already in the room, and new ideas will emerge if the conversation has a productive and positive intent. Keep reading the following chapters for more help!

WELCOME STUDENTS AS GIFTS

I was walking through school one day, visiting classes and just focusing on connecting. When I walked into a third-grade classroom, a young girl came up to me and went out of her way to introduce herself. She was articulate. She was confident. She definitely caught my attention. She told me that she was new last week and she hadn't met me yet.

I immediately felt terribly guilty. What hit me the most was that *she* came up to *me*. I pride myself on making positive relationships with students, but here was one that I hadn't even met yet in person. I realized something had to change, but I didn't know what. I don't ever want someone to feel unwelcome or that we don't care about them as individuals.

Reflecting more and considering the needs of my school community, I knew this was also a larger issue than just this one little girl. Our school is located near Washington, DC, so it is a very transient area and also has a high percentage of military-connected families. Consequently, we have students that transfer in for short periods of time and then move every three years. Our military families expressed guilt about the effect of these moves on their children, but a permanent change of station (PCS) is not a choice, it's a command, and military kids go along for the ride, sacrificing their friendships and connections along the way. I've learned that for these students, making immediate relationships is key for a smooth transition.

Despite all these kids coming and going, we didn't have a process at all to officially welcome them in during the year! We have your typical open-house and back-to-school experiences, but if a child comes in during the winter or spring, there are no fun greetings or welcome committees for them. It took a lot of discussion and brainstorming, but we ended up with a process and ultimately a new ritual that has been really special for our school, and not just for military-connected students, but like many of our best strategies, something that has been so helpful for all kids.

When a family registers with our secretaries, they set up a specific time for the family to come in on the first day with their child. They are greeted in the front office, given a gift bag that includes a school bag, T-shirt, pencil, and various knickknacks. I come out and welcome the parents and children, introducing myself and explaining what we stand for as a school. I show them our mural of shared values and ask them to agree to being kind, safe, creative, hardworking, and fun. They stand in front of this mural for a family picture, but not with me. As much as I love selfies, my goal is to make it about them, so I instead am the photographer. Before the parents leave, I print out the picture on a photo printer in my office, write a nice note on the back, and give it to them to pin up on their fridge at home.

By then, the child's new homeroom class is waiting in the main hallway to greet their new classmate. They circle up as a class, and I introduce the new parents and students into the circle. The students repeat our mottos and mantras, help explain our expected behaviors, and I challenge every single one of them to reach out and help this child that day.

I show them a magic stick and ask them to join hands, something that gets increasingly uncomfortable as the children age and mature. (Secretly, that discomfort makes me chuckle inside. As long as I can, I'm going to try and keep my students young at heart and open to something as simple as holding hands.) When all the students and adults are connected in one big circle, the magic stick glows neon and emits a sharp sound as if turning on by magic. I explain that it only lights up if we are all connected and in it for each other. The magic stick uses the electricity that flows though us and then binds us together as one team. It is such a great physical reminder of the science behind the relationships that form. It's also a neat trick!

As I introduce the parents to the teacher, I also invite the family to go visit the classroom—right there and then, no appointment needed. I ask them to review it and make sure they feel comfortable with their child's classroom and teacher. The teachers step up and go out of their way to have a welcoming attitude as well. Some make signs, some have new chants, and most have already taught the new child's name to the class. Over time this ritual has grown. Our counselors touch base with the family and set up older students as ambassadors to help with a school tour.

As you welcome your students, don't miss the opportunity to get to know them and informally assess where they may be on your class and school bell curve. The sooner we know what they need, the sooner we can line up the appropriate support. Often, with a welcoming routine like this, we are able to do this in the very first visit.

Take advantage of the moment and set the tone you want to convey. My goal is for parents and students to feel welcome and accepted, to feel that we care, and to feel that we will listen to their concerns. I find that just being an active and engaged listener is all that is needed most of the time.

Schools get one chance to make a first impression, and these experiences should be about giving new students and families a positive connection they won't soon forget. It sets the tone so that later, when you may have to have harder conversations, it's not the first time you're meeting.

Be proactive in teaching your values and vision for success on day one. These moments are opportunities to reinforce your behavioral expectations in a positive and proactive way, while also connecting them and their family to your school and its culture. These rituals are as good for your current students as they are for new students. They remind students to help others and be proactive in supporting classmates.

SEE THE POTENTIAL SUCCESS IN EVERY STUDENT

Knowing that you have students with different abilities and backgrounds helps you understand what your students may need. But awareness is only a first step. Moving from awareness into acceptance shows that we truly want the students to be in our class, not just that we're aware that they are there. For this reason, many groups, such as autistic self-advocates, have pushed for the term "acceptance" to be used over "awareness."

I asked my friend and self-advocate Conner Cummings to give me his unique perspective on this issue. Conner was taught in specialized classes for much of his academic career. He was nonverbal for much of elementary school, but he had teachers that never gave up on him, teachers who loved him for who he was and could see the potential in him.

> Demonstrating to each child that you believe in them will open the door for them to believe in themselves. Let them try things their way.
>
> Teach students how to ask for what they need in whatever way they communicate. Listen to them, whether they speak with words, typing, movement, behavior, or actions. This is ALL communication. Teach children how to invite others into their worlds. If they like a certain book, encourage others to read with them. If they like a certain toy, include that toy as a play and/or learning tool.
>
> Help us to find our passions. My fine motor skills were not strong, so I was not good in most sports and no one picked me for their team. The coach discovered that I could run and I was fast, so he included team baton races as part of PE. I learned I was a runner. He called me up to show the other children the rules of racing. When they saw how fast I was, I then became the first person picked.
>
> Search for the core of the child. Help them to find their passions. Expose them to as much as possible. Step out of your comfort zone and find a way to reach every child.

Connor always reminds me that we are dealing with real human beings. People with fears, dreams, and needs. We must start our instruction and discipline from where our students are, not where we wish they were.

> Do not exclude us because you do not think we "fit" the preconceived vision of the "typical." We may need a few

accommodations, but those tools will allow us to achieve. I was told by teachers, educator, and even a principal that I would never pass the fifth-grade level, never be able to follow more than one simple command. Never use the word "never." Do not discourage families. Presume competence.

I have grown because teachers, friends, and family believed in me. When you believe in someone, you give them tools, not walls. Teachers are like angels. They have magic in them.

Respect our autistic identities. Autistic children grow up to be autistic adults. Give us the tools that we need to survive and thrive as happy, healthy, autistic people our entire lifetimes. You are a key to our success.

Embrace what makes your kids unique and special. Kids like Conner can and will grow into adults that can shape our world if given the chance. Conner is now a national speaker and advocate for those with disabilities. He has spoken to the United Nations and in Autism Society conferences. He has a law named after him.

RELATIVE STRENGTHS AND RELATIVE WEAKNESSES

I once noticed that we never had students in special education also in gifted education. I remember one student that was behaviorally really challenging so it prevented his teachers from putting him up for gifted since he didn't "deserve" it. He missed a lot of school that year due to these behaviors, but at the end of the year, he had perfect scores on his state tests, something that few of our students achieved. He was obviously gifted. After seeing that, I put him up for the gifted program, and even filled out the recommendation form myself. That set a precedent that we would allow all our students to be identified as gifted no matter what disability they might also have. And it doesn't stop there. IEPs should list a child's strengths and reflect the whole child, so that when teachers read these plans, they get a clear picture of the student overall, not just the student's problems.

We focus way too much on only the negative side of some of our students. We have so many plans, discussions, and interventions about their problems, and the child becomes thought of as a problem child, not a child with problems. Force yourself to highlight the strengths they do have and let others know. Students with disabilities or students with other difficulties that impact their behavior or learning have *relative* strengths and weaknesses. Some of the weaknesses are so glaring that we can't see the strengths they do have. If you can't identify one strength for every child you serve, you are not looking hard enough.

Consider using a radar chart to see a more balanced view of your student. A radar chart can be used as a visual representation of the relationships between characteristics in the context of the whole child. Draw a circle on a piece of paper and add a dot in the center. The dot will represent zero. Then draw lines, or spokes, starting from the dot out to the edge of the circle, or wheel. Make one spoke for each characteristic you wish to review and label them. Draw smaller circles within the larger wheel to scale the spokes. The number can vary, but for something like characteristics, it helps to keep it simple, like 5 or 10. Use data as much as possible to decide where the levels are for each characteristic. If you don't have specific data, use a group to decide together the levels. Then connect the points together around the circle.

STRENGTHS-BASED STUDENT RADAR CHART

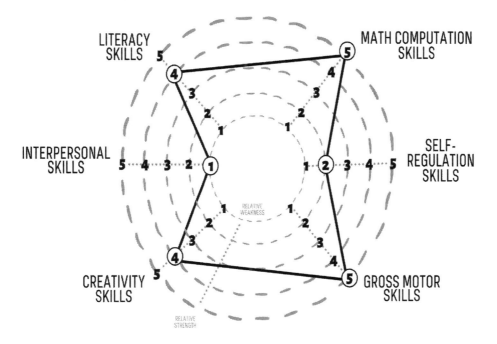

As you can see in the example, a student may be weak in interpersonal skills but very strong in math computation skills. Due to the distracting behaviors, we as educators may not be able to see the strengths emerge. Next time you are struggling with a student, take a minute to complete a radar chart to better understand the child and all their abilities. It is a great tool for showing how different skills compare to each other, and it helps put things into perspective. No child is low in everything and one of our main jobs as educators is to find something special, a strength or a gift, in every child.

Take another step and have the child fill a radar chart out about himself or herself. (Try one on your own, too, and see how your abilities look!) No one is perfect. No one is truly "well rounded," even highly successful people. The better we understand this, the more understanding and accepting we will be of all our kids.

TIME-OUT

> Analyze the birth dates of your students. Do you notice any connection to performance? Any surprises?

> What routines do you have to welcome new students into your classroom after the year has begun?

> How do you immediately set the tone for expectations? How do you get to know students as individuals?

> What strategies do you already use to quickly form relationships? What can you add?

CHAPTER 2

PREVENT FAILURE LIKE FIRST RESPONDERS

YOU BEGIN SAVING THE WORLD BY SAVING ONE PERSON AT A TIME. –CHARLES BUKOWSKI

It was one of the hotter days we'd had in a while. A 109-degree heat index. I could feel the heat sweep into the main office from the open doors at the beginning of dismissal.

Out of nowhere, a woman ran into the school, frantically shouting. It was clear she needed help as she waved us outside.

I sprinted after her through the parking lot to a small blue sedan. It quickly became clear why the woman was so panicked. She was the caregiver for one of our severely disabled students, and she'd accidentally locked the child in the car all buckled in but without the engine or air conditioning on. The girl could not unbuckle herself, unlock the doors, or roll down the windows.

On an 85-degree day, the temperature inside a car with the windows slightly open can reach 120 degrees within half an hour. It was already over 100 degrees outside, so the danger level was serious.

I quickly looked at the line of cars with parents picking up their children. The road to the school was jammed with traffic. There was no way a fire truck was going to get here in time, so I knew it was time to act.

After getting the go-ahead from the caregiver, and without giving my plan much thought, I hustled to the other side of the car and pulled out my ring of school keys from my pocket. I slammed them quickly into the window to bash it. What a dumb move. It didn't work at all and did more damage to my hands than the window.

I ran back into the front office and began shouting for a hammer. My team looked at me with part urgent concern and part "here we go again." They didn't flinch, though, and found a hammer for me right away. I ran back to the parking lot. Sliding to a stop, I took the hammer to the window on the side of the sedan farthest from the child. Feeling like Thor, god of thunder, I slammed the hammer down right in the middle of the glass. Boom!

But then it bounced right back at me. The window...didn't...break. I couldn't believe it! I'm not a little guy. I should have been able to do this. I stopped and thought for a moment, fully aware that the child was desperately waiting, the car was heating up, and the students and families around me were trying to figure out what in the heck I was doing. I looked closer at the window and noticed the slight curve it had to it. I had been hitting the middle of the window—its strongest part.

I swung again, with humility and extra effort, but aiming for the lower corner. This time the window smashed into a million pieces. I reached in, unlocked the car, and helped unbuckle the girl from her seat. I could feel how hot it was in that car. One of our secretaries reached in and carried the girl to the office to cool her down. Her mother arrived soon after and embraced her child with love and thankfulness.

I was proud to be able to help, but the reality is that I got lucky. I wasn't really prepared. Again. New situation, but felt like déjà vu, not being prepared for my students. I didn't know what to do or how to help. I realized that I should have been more ready to take the right kind of action during a crisis like this. I love to think of myself as a first responder, running into the danger for my students, but I realized that day that I better train like one, too.

EDUCATORS ARE FIRST RESPONDERS, TOO

If you talk to a first responder like a firefighter, police officer, or medic, they describe their work as who they are, not just something they do. They have an air about them that makes it clear they are ready and willing to take action at a moment's notice. They fight to save every last person they can. They come across as having a calling for their work, like it means something really important to them deep down.

Sounds familiar, right? It should. Educators are first responders, too.

Emergencies in schools are not just about shootings and physical alterations. We have many crises every day: a child not learning to how to read, not having friends, not being able to function properly in society; students telling us that they are having suicidal thoughts or are being abused; or a child being grade levels below in reading, which statistically correlates to an extremely high likelihood of future incarceration. These are situations that demand our immediate and undivided attention, real emergencies we face in schools that we need to be ready and willing to handle.

We deal with life-and-death situations, even though many times we consider them merely as the normal workings of a typical school day. The average person has no idea what educators really deal with on an everyday basis. We need to be ready and alert to deal with trauma, conflicts, and the wildest of circumstances. Explain these situations to those outside education and they wouldn't think it normal at all.

Emergencies don't wait for you to get ready. We must be mentally and physically ready to deal with our toughest situations head on, even if we don't know what exactly to do yet. The mindset and readiness of a first responder must be there *before* these emergencies occur. Running into the fire to put it out and save others is a great attitude, but if you aren't careful, you'll end up trying to put it out with gasoline or just getting yourself hurt. Just like first responders, we need to use the right tool for the job and prepare for the situations we can predict. Most of being prepared is getting our minds right. Then we need to prepare with training and practice so that when these emergencies occur in our school—and they will—we will be ready.

In our school, I surprise my entire staff with a field trip to kick off every school year. I tell them to wear tennis shoes, put on the new annual school T-shirt, and get on the bus. Not knowing where they are going adds to the buzz and excitement. I've arranged visits to baseball stadiums, monuments, and even space shuttles. One year, the trip took us to the largest fire station in the area. Once we got off the bus that day and after our teachers got over their surprise, the firefighters gave us lessons and insights into how they prepare for emergencies. They timed how fast they could put on their equipment. They practiced with the fire hose for accuracy and safety. They showed us the Jaws of Life and how they use them to save people from smashed-in vehicles. Then it was our turn, timing ourselves, trying out the equipment, and getting a feel for what they do. Seeing their mentality and sense of urgency firsthand was so powerful, and useful when thinking about our own craft as educators. I was so impressed with how dedicated they were and how they focused on details, like measuring their response times to the second.

CHARACTERISTICS OF FIRST RESPONDERS

First responders think, act, and plan differently than your average person. Let's break those characteristics down and consider which of them we have now. How are you a first responder in your classroom, alert and ready to help your students in a moment's notice?

Focus

First responders focus on saving one person at a time. They know there are limitations on their focus and energy, and they give it their all for the person that needs it the most at any given time. Educators have so much responsibility for their students, and teachers feel an enormous amount of pressure to help every child be successful. It can be debilitating. Overwhelming. One way to help yourself is to focus your mind on only one student at a time. This may sound contrary to the 100-percent mindset ensuring success for all, but, in fact, it's the only way to really help all kids. Intensely focus on the needs of one student at a time or your energy will be scattered and you won't be effective. This doesn't mean that you can only focus on one student for the year. It means that you must be intentional with your time and energy throughout the day. Teach in the moment and stay intensely focused.

Empathy

To be an effective first responder, you must have empathy toward others. Empathy isn't sympathy. Empathy is imagining what someone else is going through emotionally and physically as if it were happening to ourselves. Educators all say they care about their students, but empathy is really what we should feel. When we place ourselves in this mindset, we act in a more proactive manner and are better at providing support or next steps, because we can feel how our actions will affect our students. We can also imagine how it would feel if we did nothing for our students. This helps educators think of their students' overall needs, not just academic- or standards-based needs. Dealing with problems turns into a mission to help instead of a box to check off so we can get back to the "lesson." We often find that there is more going on than the immediate problem at hand when we ask questions and dig deeper, but you only do that when you care. The more we get to know students and their home lives, friendship groups, and needs, the better we will be able to intervene when the time comes. Set aside time to talk with them individually—about them, not about academics or behaviors. Use reflection sheets to help them articulate things that may be bothering them. Learn more to do more.

Initiative

First responders step up when others just stand and look. They act even if they don't know exactly what to do. They act because they know that doing nothing is always worse. In schools, we constantly *admire* problems in meetings or in the hallways. We are experts at telling you what is wrong, so much so that we even create countless forms for breaking these problems down in detail. Principals can sit in meetings, look at spreadsheets, and listen to all the problems of the school, and end up not really helping at all. I'm as guilty of this as anyone else. We need to put this effort into direct actions instead. It's so important to get out of our chairs and go directly to the person who needs help. Even if you just go and generally support a classroom activity or sit with a student, action will be appreciated. When in doubt, just go do something.

Solution Orientation

First responders think differently when working together or facing problems. They don't have time for second-guessing motivations and perseverating on problems. In education, we use the phrase "No shame, no blame," but we often do exactly that—shame and blame others instead of working only toward solutions. When firefighters or medics come on a scene, they act for the good of the group, not just their own self-interest. They tend to be more positive and show a can-do attitude. They tend to not complain and bring up all the potential problems. Instead, they are focused on how to assist and identify a potential solution. Focusing on problems is a vicious cycle that no one wins. Learn about the problem only enough to figure out next steps.

Readiness

An effective first responder is not expected to know everything about everything, but they are expected to know their field very well. They are expected to study and train with best practices, so that when called upon, they can do the best work. Educators should do the same, constantly learn and refine practices to become experts in their field, ready to give advice or learn more when they don't know the answers, and never be satisfied with thinking they already know all there is to know. Evaluate your school by observing the most experienced educators in the building. Schools with thirty-year teachers that are still constantly learning and growing even as they look toward retirement are the schools that are most prepared for students. That shared mindset and attitude is contagious to others, and new teachers look to these building leaders for how they should conduct themselves.

Reliability

Having the best skills isn't enough. You must be reliable to others when they need you. Reliability is probably one of the most underrated characteristics. When we think of our first responders, we think of them being there for us anytime we need them. Being reliable for students is imperative. They need to know that you will always be there when they need you and that they can count on you to follow through. We have too many educators that do amazing work, but for many different reasons, are not there for their students or colleagues. Sometimes this is because of a simple lack of consistency. Sometimes it's because of a conflict with their personal lives. Sometimes their work ethic isn't strong enough. Our students can't afford for us to be 100 percent some days and 20 percent other days. What if one of those days they were falling apart and needed to be picked back up, but we weren't ready or willing to do that? You can't be all in for kids if you aren't ready to go every day.

Courage

First responders face their fears with courage and conviction. They know that what they are doing is important, so they will work through their fears to achieve the desired outcome. Educators often fear failure. This fear holds us back from becoming our true, best selves. Courage only exists with fear because it means overcoming this fear. If the challenge in front of you is scary, you're probably on the right path. If you have a challenging situation that keeps you up at night and makes you cry out of frustration, know that you are not alone. The courage that first responders have comes from their shared experiences and knowing that others have their back. Gain strength from the team around you. Have go-to friends you can count on in your lives to keep you on track.

Bravery Requires Fear

Don't ever forget that you are human and are not expected to be unafraid. Just don't let fear stop you from moving forward. One trick is to write down the thing that scares you the most in the situation. Look at it and consider what that fear really means. Most of the time we make more out of it than it deserves. Once you write down that fear, you can come up with a plan to tackle it head on. Are you afraid of losing control? Of looking like you don't know what you are doing? Are you afraid that your student will hate you if you press too hard? Let those fears drive you to plan for changes in your schedule to build a positive relationship using individual time and attention beyond the instructional strategies you are pushing.

STUDENT BEHAVIORS ARE THE ALARM BELLS RINGING

Occasionally, we find ourselves in situations where we must act quickly and trust our gut instincts. Sometimes the answers are obvious. Most times, though, the issues we deal with are complicated and the next steps are not so clear.

Students who display glaring misbehaviors in your school are like blaring alarms going off, warning you of danger. Students have enormous pressures from their families, society, and schools. They also have immediate access to the most dangerous and negative influences in society right now. We are the educators there for our kids no matter what they bring. We are their first responders, often literally the first on the scene for their school crises.

ZONE OF PROXIMAL DEVELOPMENT

Promoting struggle and guiding students to solutions is key to growing students forward. Child psychologist Lev Vygotsky stated that growth occurs most effectively in a person's zone of proximal development. This describes a range where a skill is too difficult for the person to master independently but not too difficult for that person to learn with guidance, encouragement, and instruction.

We all need support and guidance through the learning process regardless of the new skill we are trying to master. When students feel as if they are on their own and not making progress, they lose hope. Only if they have hope that they can keep moving forward in a skill will they keep trying with meaningful effort.

For educators, providing the right supports at the right time is key in helping students while they struggle and to prevent failure and frustration. This means we have to know our students really well, their strengths and weaknesses, especially those of students who tend to struggle more often. Many students, like many adults, must overcome enormous obstacles caused by external factors such as poverty, abuse, and trauma. Life is not easy, and our students need to learn resiliency and determination during times of adversity. The trick is not to let them break.

We give students hope and the will to keep trying (instead of disrupting) through giving them support and tools. Giving the gift of hope is more than just words. Kids want to see real results to truly believe that they can get better. More specifically, any success will lead to more success in the future. Instead of focusing on problems or concerns, realign your energy to create small wins or recognize ones already happening around you. If you are stuck and don't know what to do, just stop. Find one little area of improvement.

Helping our students remember times they were successful and changing the way they think about their own struggles will have an impact on their future behaviors. Teach students to reflect: connect a discouraging struggle they had in the past, even a small one, to how they overcame it and then ultimately became successful. This will help them build confidence in their own patterns of achievement.

Like pushing a heavy boulder, the beginning stages of success are always the most difficult. Get that thing rolling and it gets easier and easier to keep it moving. And then it's hard to stop it from going in the right direction. Momentum is a powerful tool to build confidence and self-efficacy in our students. The way to help kids to see progress is to monitor it, celebrate it, and show them that you value their efforts.

What if your student has never been successful? First, that's unlikely. Second, you've hit the nail on the head. That's *exactly* what we need to focus on most: how can we help a student who feels like a failure find any little bit of success? Little wins are the foundation for an upward trend in positive outcomes.

THE FAILURE MYTH

FAIL, or "first attempt in learning," is a popular idea in education right now, but I think it's wrong, or at least a little misguided. The FAIL acronym was coined by Dr. Abdul Kalam and is used so often that it is one of the first things to pop up when you search online for the word fail. The FAIL model is often illustrated with examples of Albert Einstein failing math, Bill Gates dropping out of college, or Michael Jordan getting cut from his varsity basketball team, all before achieving greatness. These stories are used to demonstrate that highly successful people have failed and that their failures helped them to become more successful.

The idea that promoting failure will actually help kids succeed is a myth. I know this can be a difficult thing to read, especially if you have these posters already up in your classroom, but hear me out. Alfie Kohn, author and lecturer on human behavior, education, and parenting, explained well myth of "productive failure" in a great article titled *The Failure of Failure*. He wrote, "The question is how likely it is that failure will be productive. And the answer is: Not very. The benefits of screwing up are wildly overrated. What's most reliably associated with successful outcomes, it turns out, are prior experiences with success, not with failure. While there are exceptions, the most likely consequence of having failed at something is that children will come to see themselves as lacking competence."[1]

The fact is that failure is highly stressful and scarring, particularly to students who are already feeling beleaguered. Failures can have very negative side effects on them emotionally. We should be teaching students how *not* to fail, not promoting failure itself.

The myth that failing is good for kids is exacerbated by the many struggles that our students have in their daily lives and in their traumatic experiences. Failure in some ways is inevitable, but we should do everything we can for those in our care to minimize its impact.

---

1   Alfie Kohn, "The Failure of Failure," June 23, 2016, alfiekohn.org/blogs/failure/.

Catching Students before They Fall (and Fail)

No single strategy is best for helping students in any given area. Teachers will be more successful when they align their strategies to how the child is doing and what they will need next. That means that we need to do our homework and keep learning new behavioral strategies. Create a bank of strategies and save links to online resources so that you can have a variety of tools at your disposal. Never throw your hands up and say that you've tried everything. Know where to go to get more ideas and help.

If something matters to you and helps your students, it should be something that you do every day. Remember we are first responders. Consistency and redundancy matters. Every year, the fire department and/or the school district's central office team conducts multiple inspections to check the fire extinguishers, the exits, and anything else considered essential for safety. Even if things seem to be working fine, these items are checked with a sense of urgency, even having names and dates written down to confirm they were done. Why? Because it's literally life and death and it matters.

Checking the social-emotional status of your students should thought of in the same way. It's life and death and it matters. Prepare a routine of asking students how they feel as you start your day or your class lessons. Do this carefully and thoughtfully, without putting students on the spot.

There are many ways to do this, especially with the emergence of online access for students. One way is to have students come in, let them take a sticky note, write their name on the sticky side, and then place it on a section of your board, wall, or an easel near the door. The board is broken up into different sections such as "I feel good," "I'm OK," "I feel sad," and "I need help." Because the names are on the inside of the stickies, the students won't see their peers' responses. The section labels can be adjusted to make them more age appropriate, perhaps with symbols instead of words, or you can use prepared name cards and slots/shelves for sections.

DAILY CHECK-IN

I'M GREAT!

....

I'M OKAY

....

I'M HAVING A ROUGH DAY

....

I'M REALLY STRUGGLING

Another way to do check in with students is through apps like Padlet, Flipgrid, or Zoom. Use a range for students to pick from instead of leaving it open ended. For instance, on a scale of . . . Disney characters, Marvel characters, or puppies. Then students can see the visuals laid out in child-friendly images, memes, and GIFs for them to choose from. Are they upset, happy, or nervous? In any case, it's important for the teacher to know. Share a screen that allows students to rate their feelings and privately notify you of what help they need. Video submissions allow you to speak privately with students to provide aid when consistent in-person conversations are not achievable. Use systems to create checks on students through their behaviors, downward trends in academic scores, and input from parents, peers, and mentors.

The most efficient way, though, to find out students' emotional levels is to ask them simply and directly. We often do everything but talk individually with students to learn how they are doing. We can't rely on chance and luck to find crucial information about a student. Don't just ask, "How are you feeling?" No one knows how to answer that. Ask better questions that can help you gain insight. Be intentional with questions like these instead: On a scale of one to ten, how is your day? Why? What strengths do you bring to this world? What is one thing holding you back from your goals right now? If you could improve school in one way, what would that be? What is one thing you wish you could be better at doing? What was the best part of your week so far? Why?

Getting kids talking and allowing themselves to be vulnerable is key.

Asking for Students

Effective discipline is proactive. You know your school is going in the right direction when you have teachers fight for the privilege of working with the most challenging students.

When you shift your attitude to celebrate new students as gifts and challenges, you realize that each new student is an opportunity. That helps you be happy as much as it helps the students feel welcome.

Don't just listen to me. One of my teachers, Kristin Keskel, has this attitude already, and she's one of the leaders in our school who inspires us to take on every challenge. Here's what Kristin has to say:

> Embrace those students whose names have been repeated as a challenge. Those are the students that you need to build your relationship with quickly that first week of school; that relationship will be the building block of success when things get tough throughout the year. At the

end of the day, every parent and every child just wants to know that you love the child and care about them as a family.

We have to have high expectations for success with all of our students. Success could be achieving a certain reading level, passing a standardized test, reaching a consistent behavior goal, or getting the needed services that help a child to feel more excited and confident about learning.

Every student deserves a teacher that actually wants them in their class. And kids can tell the difference.

COMMUNICATION

First responders deal with complex problems and must communicate clearly and accurately to help each other take the essential next steps in a timely manner. Schools should think of their protocols and communication strategies the same way, especially when emergencies occur. Work these out now while things are quiet, because when they get intense, you'll be glad you did. Take it seriously.

When we care about all kids in our school, we are looking and listening to every student that we come across. We can be everywhere at once if we do this as a team. We can see fights brewing or see students isolating themselves. We can act faster.

You don't have to be perfect, but you do have be clear on how you communicate during crises to get them resolved faster and more effectively. We now do daily radio checks when school starts each day so we know we are all synced for communication. Our secretaries call out people by name one by one. Don't take for granted that everyone is ready to go for emergencies, you need to think ahead, check ahead, and get on the same page *before* any potential problem occurs.

This suggestion was given to me by one of our parents who is an Air Force veteran, and it came in useful in an emergency when a student eloped from the classroom. All of a sudden, our day turned into a red alert. Life-and-death potential. Word got out quickly through the radio that one of our fourth graders was missing. This is one of the most gut-wrenching things you can hear as a principal. The kind of news that makes you literally drop everything and just feel like you have to do something immediately, even if you don't know what exactly that is.

Because of our radio readiness, all it took was a few sentences describing the situation before everyone not with kids at that time stepped up to help. Our secretaries stationed themselves by the phones and watching the school cameras. I ran out front to check the parking lot. I turned around and suddenly I saw our whole staff coming out of the school doors, each intensely checking the areas around them. One teacher called out that the back playground was clear, another radioed in that the side parking lot was clear. We searched the building and the surrounding area. One teacher was knee deep in the woods next door. Finally, someone called in that they found the student, and that he had been inside hiding the entire time.

Many administrators would be mad at that kind of situation and the distraction it caused. I was proud. It still gives me goosebumps when I think of it. Life gave us a test, and our staff passed with flying colors.

When things get tough, communicate, communicate, communicate.

TALKING BUT NOT COLLABORATING

How many meetings do we have that make us feel like nothing was accomplished? How many long discussions do we have with our colleagues in the hallway or in class after school about the problem behaviors? It's OK to vent and to unwind, but be careful not to admire the problem instead of working toward real solutions.

Over the years, I've learned the hard way how important it is to have a clear and transparent process for teachers to receive help from administration and the rest of the school staff. Administrators can be very defensive and push blame on teachers when things don't work out perfect in the classrooms. I'm ashamed to say I've been there, and it can be a constant struggle if we aren't careful. When we end up meeting with teachers to support them instead of blaming them, there are a few key elements to make sure that meetings help a whole team better align their goals:

- Set the stage before the meeting so people are prepared with what information they need.
- Validate their situation and concerns. They obviously care about the child, which is why they are in the room with you in the first place.
- Immediately create goals. Stop talking, start doing. Clearly articulate the desired behaviors.
- Create a plan of action that is real and show a sense of urgency that matches the need for change.

No one likes to feel like they aren't supported, and it's on all of us to help keep each other in check with this. There are a lot of valid reasons—and also excuses—for why the collaboration breaks down, but there are solutions. Create a specific process that teachers can use when they need help, one that is focused on solutions and support. Don't make teachers prove they need help or make them feel like a problem is their fault. At our school, through a team effort from our reading teachers, school counselors, and administrators, we've created a process called Student Focus Groups that employs some important tools:

Simple request forms: Forms can be dreadful, but they are a necessity. Keep things simple, and only ask for what you really need to know before a meeting.

Script meetings: It helped us to create sentence starters for the teachers that were requesting help so that we could guide them in a way that was productive. We also needed scripts and talking points so that we stayed positive and helpful, without blaming the teacher. If you go in with no real plan, the worst habits tend to take over. Be prepared.

Meeting notes: Assign one person to note details of the problem behavior, potential root causes, what has worked, and what the teacher needs help with next.

Problem solvers: The attitude of the group is important. This is a problem-solving and helpful team. No shame. No blame. Have resources for additional strategies readily available. We're all in it together. The goal is for the teacher to leave feeling like they were supported and walk away with practical strategies they can use.

Follow-through: Checklists and plans need to be created right then and there. If you know you have a process the child needs, add it now. Don't wait. Don't give the teacher homework. Get it done. Follow-through is often where things fall apart. Fix this by having templates for next steps available during a meeting that can be completed and sent out right away.

DEBRIEFING

Another partnership in our school with a parent led to unique training and experiences for me and our staff. This started with federal law enforcement officer Chris Lee, also one of our parents, asking to use our school as a practice facility for his team to practice their response to an active-shooter incident. What started as an interesting learning experience observing and learning from real life heroes ended up as over half a dozen active-shooter trainings also involving my buddy and principal Hamish Brewer. We became almost part of the team and were about as hands-on and actively involved as you can get. Add Hamish and I into the mix and you know we will go all in no matter what's asked of us!

Working with the best of the best like this, there are so many things we can glean and incorporate into our work as educational leaders. We felt humbled and honored to be included on their team. What educators should know, though, is that they were so appreciative in their recognition of our work as well. Hold your head up. You are looked at as heroes, too.

One thing that stuck out during these trainings was how the team communicated with each other in open and challenging dialogue, something we talk about needing more of in education, but also struggle to ensure happens regularly. At the end of each training scenario, they circled up for a debriefing they called a "hot wash," even adding Hamish and I into the group. Here's how Chris describes it:

> After every run or exercise in the school, our team would gather for a quick "hot wash," where we dissected the run and identified our mistakes and areas of improvement. A law enforcement tactical team is a tight-knit group of people who work together very closely and trust each other implicitly, yet also have a thick skin. The success of the team and our individual safety rests on the ability of each team member to do their job quickly and expertly.
>
> We recognize that training days are the time to address any deficiencies, make mistakes, and fix them. Accordingly, our hot wash sessions can appear blunt to the outsider, yet no one gets offended. A team member who makes a mistake or deviates from an established tactic will openly acknowledge it and offer it as a learning point for the team. In other instances, team members will bluntly ask someone what they were doing or why they made a specific decision—and expect an answer. We recognize that training days are the time to make mistakes and fix them so they don't happen in live operations when the cost is much, much higher.

The focus of these hot wash sessions is on the tactics and execution, not the person themselves. Accordingly, no one gets offended or upset, even though the conversation is blunt and to the point. Mistakes are identified, solutions are offered, and we repeat the run to fix the issue. We all recognize that none of us are infallible. Instead, we rely on those we trust to point out our shortcomings and help us achieve a higher level or performance.

What if we could guarantee a "hot wash" after each disciplinary situation that occurred in the classroom? Instead of complaining and blaming in the hallways, think of the benefit that an open and honest process like this would be both to our own well-being and to the solutions we could find for our students!

DO SOMETHING ENOUGH AND YOU BECOME IT

The more you act like the thing you want to be, the more you become it. If you want to be a hero, it starts by acting like one. How do you think first responders all felt when they first started? Do you think they all felt ready? No way. Ask them next time they are in your school. Learn from firefighters and police officers when they visit for safety lessons. Do what they do. Think how they think. Act like what you are doing every day is life-and-death serious. You'll start realizing that you aren't acting. Others will start looking at you differently. Our work as educators *is* that serious. It matters.

Educators are first responders. We are there on the front lines when our students face some of their most difficult challenges. This mindset will help you because it drives a deeper purpose and meaning in our work. You. Are. A. Hero. If you think of yourself that way every day, how will your actions and attitudes shift accordingly?

Students often misbehave due to feeling like failures academically and socially. If we watch closely and have strategies in place, we can intervene to catch them as they fall. What greater gift than to be truly ready for a student who needs you?

TIME-OUT

> Many schools incorporate programs with local first responders, but do you learn from them and change or improve your practices accordingly? How could you take one step more to learn more about how they run their organization?

> How do you currently debrief in your school with your colleagues? Is it talking in the hallway after school? Is it in a special meeting?

CHAPTER 3

ALIGN DISCIPLINE WITH LONG-TERM GOALS

DISCIPLINE IS A CHOICE. IT'S SIMPLY CONSISTENTLY CHOOSING THE HARD RIGHT OVER THE EASY WRONG. —RORY VADEN

"Slackers!"

That's the catchphrase of Mr. Strickland, the principal in the eighties classic *Back to the Future*, and it jibes exactly with his buttoned-up suit, bow tie, and air of authority. You could tell that he was just waiting to pounce on any student that steps out of line and make lives life miserable.

The tough, uncompromising, humorless disciplinarian whose approach was based in fear was a popular depiction in eighties movies, with characters like Mr. Strickland, Mr. Rooney from *Ferris Bueller's Day Off*, and Mr. Vernon from *The Breakfast Club,* who threatened his students that he would crack their skulls if they didn't shape up. Many of us grew up with these "models," and assumed that's what discipline was supposed to be. And, like in many other aspects of our society, it's difficult to know if the art reflected the reality or the reality acted out the art.

It's clear, though, that these characters were the bad guys, and we can learn what not to do from their examples. Their actions did nothing to establish positive relationships and instead encouraged their students to manipulate situations and find loopholes. Characters like Marty McFly or Ferris Bueller were fun to watch precisely because they could play the game, acting appropriately only when directly in front of an administrator. They never acted in the right way because they wanted to—only because they didn't want to get caught.

These characters, while fictional, also represented a common form of discipline that many of us grew up knowing as the way school discipline was supposed to be. The eighties weren't the only time that we saw this style of discipline. There's a tradition in our country of shame, punishment, and exclusion that continues even today.

Before we move into why these traditional practices don't work and what you can do instead, think about how these characters must have felt about themselves and their jobs on a daily basis. They didn't seem happy or fulfilled. They seemed angry and upset. They were trying to "catch" kids misbehaving.

That's no way to live! Teachers and administrators that walk around trying to catch misbehavior will find it wherever they look. The same is true for those that look for positive actions. Which are you? "I caught you" is a slippery and dangerous slope, often self-fulfilling. "I caught you" celebrates failure. "I got you" celebrates progress. The former is practically excited when the students meet their expectation of misconduct. The latter is about supporting students even if they are acting in ways that don't show they even want it. It recognizes unconditional positive regard and is excited over any level of forward momentum.

We can find much more meaning and inspiration if we choose a more positive and productive course.

SHEDDING TRADITIONAL DISCIPLINE PRACTICES THAT DON'T WORK

While we want to be nice to our students, of course we need to keep our expectations for their behavior high and maintain a sense of order. The best educators have a sense of "tough love." They aren't push-overs. "Tough love" means being tough in our work but implementing discipline with love for our students and care for their well-being.

Traditional strategies to address misconduct didn't always take this approach. Historically, in both society as a whole and in schools, the idea of consequence-driven (sometimes corporal) punishment has been pervasive in how we treat people who violate rules or break laws. But that mentality simply doesn't work. And this isn't just me saying or thinking that; the research speaks for itself.

I understand that, at different levels, there are behaviors that cannot be tolerated and will have natural consequences—especially ones that break laws involving drugs, weapons, and serious violence—but we have to change our mindset about making examples of our kids or showing them "who's the boss." Even serious acts should not always have automatic consequences if we know they will not work to improve the behavior we are trying to change.

Whether you are a teacher dealing with the daily issues of a classroom or an administrator juggling what to do for each new situation that comes up in your office, each of us has our own journey in this area. My journey was largely an evolution that resulted from seeing what worked and what didn't work over time. Automatic exclusions in the form of office time-outs, suspensions, and detentions were just not working. They didn't change behavior and instead turned everything into a fight, not just between students, but eventually between teachers and parents, with no one seeming to be satisfied with any of the next steps.

Why was everyone upset? I came to realize that it came down to one thing: lack of improvement. Teachers just wanted things to get better. The vast majority of teachers are loving and kind, not wanting to get kids in trouble, but they do want to see bad behavior addressed and improved. And rightly so. Parents feel the same way. No matter how defensive we can be as parents, myself included, we want our kids to behave and be respectful. But we also don't want them to be treated with disrespect themselves or with overly harsh disciplinary practices that humiliate or ostracize.

So what do we do?

We're educators. Our superpower is learning and helping others learn. So I dug in to the research. What I learned changed my entire philosophy on school discipline and created a new core belief: Exclusions and punitive consequences do more harm than good. And I will not in any way intentionally harm my students. Therefore, I don't believe in using suspensions anymore. I haven't suspended a student in years, and it's not because we haven't had serious misconduct. I'm in a real school with real issues.

There are some really convincing reasons why we should think more progressively and differently on this issue. Why shouldn't we suspend students? How can we handle these situations instead?

Public Education Is Meant for All

Public education in America is meant to educate and support every child. We want them all to be included, regardless of income, background, race, ability, immigration status, or gender. We should have enormous pride in this and carry it like a badge of honor. We'll take as many students as we can no matter what they look like, what language they speak, or what issues they bring with them. We don't discriminate. We educate. No questions asked. We don't just accept students, we welcome them with open arms.

Schooling has not always been this way, though. It hasn't even always been mandatory for children. In the nineteenth century, only rich kids could go to school. In the early twentieth century, states individually agreed to mandate public education—for white children. It took an entire national Civil Rights Movement and a monumental Supreme Court Case, Brown v. Board of Education in 1954, to allow Black students into the same public schools as white students. The argument, rightly so, was that if education was a public right, then it should be available to all children, no matter the color of their skin. This push for desegregation started the wave of inclusion we are still riding today.

School has changed in many significant and dramatic ways in a very short amount of time. Parents and teachers alike make statements about wishing for school to get back to the good old days, when discipline was tough and there were consequences for kids' actions. That's a phrase we should question any time we hear it: the "good old days" were not very good for most people. Large groups of our current students, especially students of color and students with disabilities, would have been socially and legally discriminated against throughout most of our school history. These were definitely *not* the good old days.

When you look at your student body, think about the differences that make your school special. We should continue to advocate and ensure that marginalized students and their families have the rights they deserve. Even now, many students do not have equal access to education. This must be considered as we investigate the increasing number of discipline challenges that we face.

National surveys and studies show that Black and Hispanic students are suspended more often, at higher rates, and for longer periods of time than white students for the same behaviors. The increased time out of class only exacerbates the problem.

If students of color are kicked out of your school at a significantly higher rate than white students, your school doesn't need an improvement plan, there needs to be a change in culture. It's not enough just to add a committee. There's a massive problem that needs to be treated with the sense of urgency that it deserves. Disparities in discipline like this are a slap in the face of the enormous civil rights efforts of past generations.

Unfortunately, exclusion starts early in many students' academic careers. At a shockingly early age, students begin to be excluded from their peers as a form of discipline. Preschool and kindergarten have some of the highest suspensions rates of any grade level. Students receive time-outs, are moved away from peers, and sent into hallways by themselves, often unsupervised.

Our job as classroom and school leaders is not just to make sure kids attend school but also to do everything we can to keep them here every day. It's in both the individual student's and in our society's best interest.

Special Education Is Based on Inclusion

The US Department of Education regularly reports out national statistics on exclusionary discipline. The most recent report, "An Overview of Exclusionary Discipline Practices in Public Schools for the 2017-18 School Year" describes a small decrease in the amount of exclusionary discipline, but a significant increase in the use of school-related arrests, expulsions, and referrals to law enforcement. It also reports out how students with disabilities—despite the push for inclusive practices—continue to be suspended at almost twice the rate of their nondisabled peers. It's even worse when you break down the data by race, with Black students with disabilities receiving three times as many in-school suspensions and four times as many out-of-school suspensions. This is happening even with extra plans, supports, and resources in place to address misbehaviors.[1]

Many people don't realize the connection between special education and the Civil Rights Movement that sparked special education laws

---

1   United States Department of Education Office for Civil Rights, "An Overview of Exclusionary Discipline Practices in Public Schools for the 2017–2018 School Year," June 2021, www2. ed.gov/about/offices/list/ocr/docs/crdc-exclusionary-school-discipline.pdf.

in the first place. Almost two million students with disabilities were excluded from public school before laws were enacted in the 1970s to mandate access. Most students were being serviced in institutions or were forced to stay at home. Educators in the past expressed fear of the behaviors and needs of these students, concerned with how they would affect their schools and classrooms. Some states had strict laws to exclude students considered "crippled," "feeble-minded," or "emotionally disturbed." Even as far back as 1893, courts allowed schools to exclude students for excessive drooling, for making unusual noises, and for distractions in the learning environment. These students were considered lost causes who couldn't learn and were only capable of disturbing teachers and other of the students.

In the 1970s, federal special education law was enacted, not only allowing students with disabilities into schools but also mandating equal access to education. This is where Free Appropriate Public Education (FAPE) comes into the conversation. Laws changed, granting students the right to be in school despite any behavioral challenges or disabilities they may bring with them.

WHEN WE INTENTIONALLY EXCLUDE STUDENTS FOR BEHAVIORS THAT ARE RELATED TO THEIR DISABILITY, WE ARE GOING COMPLETELY AGAINST THE INTENT OF SPECIAL EDUCATION LAW.

I want to make this point crystal clear: Special education law was written to ensure that students with disabilities were included in school. Students who receive special education are legally entitled to clearly targeted behavioral goals, instruction, and support to address their misconduct. When we intentionally exclude students for behaviors that are related to their disability, we are going completely against the intent of special education law.

Zero-Tolerance Policies Skew Discipline

Zero tolerance reflects a reflexive desire for automatic consequences and a wish to get back to the perceived good old days of discipline, when kids had consequences and schools had more authority. It is a call back to an imagined picture of traditional discipline of students sitting quietly in rows, in perfect order and paying complete attention while teachers lecture from the front of the room.

Actually, research clearly shows that zero-tolerance policies are a major reason for the significant increase overall in exclusions and the increase in the disparities between racial groups often described as the "school-to-prison pipeline."

Zero tolerance treats every student with the same exclusionary form of discipline regardless of the situation or the student's background or needs. This mindset has become entrenched into our current disciplinary policies. Most people don't realize that zero tolerance began in the 1980s in Texas as a push to stop drug cartels creeping into the schools. Zero-tolerance policies targeted and mandated expulsions for major infractions involving drugs, weapons, and serious violence. This quickly became a national staple for handling not only gang violence but even the pettiest behaviors in school.

Frighteningly, zero-tolerance policies also led to an increase in exclusions for students of color, with consequences doled out without considerations of implicit bias, cultural differences, or even of racism from staff. When someone spits out a line about the need for zero tolerance, know your facts and help them understand that what they are advocating is actually harmful for kids.

It's led to a significant increase in removals from school even for minor infractions such as bringing nail clippers to school or possessing cough drops due to a perceived and remote connection to drugs or weapons. Some of the largest school districts across the country have studied their rates and causes of suspensions working to make their own reductions. They found that over half of their suspensions were due to minor offenses such as basic school rule violations, defiance, truancy, and even cell phone usage. Since zero-tolerance policies began, studies have witnessed not only a significant increase in usage of suspensions, but also an increase in school violence, the perception that school is not safe, and laws to protect students from unfairly being excluded. The trend has reversed to head in the right direction, with districts and states creating new legal mandates to monitor, reduce, and in some cases, eliminate suspension as an option for misconduct.[2]

Exclusionary Discipline Is Not Effective

School discipline should be used to accomplish two major outcomes: one, to maintain a safe and effective learning environment for students every day, and, two, to redirect and prevent misconduct by teaching students alternative actions they can take in the future in similar situations. One would hope that the use of suspensions was a means to do just this—keep the school safe and change negative behaviors—but the results have been the opposite. When students are punished into submission, they are not learning how to be better; they only learn what not to do, and eventually they will learn to rebel against that as well.

The roots of exclusion as a form of discipline are deep and pervasive. Exclusion comes in many forms such as suspensions, time-outs in the office, being excluded from field trips and school activities, sitting in the hallway, and having a chair or desk in the corner of the room. Even in the primary grades, where educators know that students have had very little or no schooling beforehand, there is a very low tolerance for misbehavior that is very predictable. Exclusions like moving students to a seat in the corner, putting them in the hallway, sending them to another classroom for the day, and walking them to the office continue to be the norm for how discipline is handled there.

Suspension from school is one of the most common forms of exclusion and is probably listed in every school's code of behavior or discipline handbook. Suspension is based on the idea that when

---

2 Curran, F., "Estimating the Effect of State Zero Tolerance Laws on Exclusionary Discipline, Racial Discipline Gaps, and Student Behavior," *Educational Evaluation and Policy Analysis, 38* (4), 2016, 647–668.

students step out of line, we exclude them from school to send a message to them and their peers that the behaviors they are exhibiting are not acceptable. It puts pressure on parents and puts a record of the infraction in their school file. These consequences are meant to warn others and prevent them from exhibiting the same misbehaviors in the future.

Considering how much this tool is used, one would assume that it's a really effective strategy to improve behavior, right? The reality is much different. There is no evidence that suspensions help change behavior or even make the school feel safer. Suspensions and exclusions do not improve misbehavior, but instead they actually have many negative effects associated with them. If you suspend a child, you are making their lives and outcomes worse, not better. This was the biggest shock for me when I did my own research in this area.

Daniel Losen and Russell Skiba have written powerful research articles such as "From Reaction to Prevention: Turning the Page on School Discipline." These clearly explain the negative effects over time for students when using exclusionary discipline. Also, an increase in exclusionary discipline does not increase the rates of stakeholder satisfaction in their school climate nor decrease the rates of student misconduct. Suspension reinforces future misbehavior, with students more likely to be suspended again, drop out, or become subject to the juvenile justice system. Students miss additional academic instruction when they are excluded from school and class, which causes them to fall farther behind their peers.[3] The American Pediatrics Association has made it clear that schools must reduce suspensions and that schools with higher rates of exclusionary discipline were not safer for their students or staff.[4]

Suspensions are one of the most serious consequences that schools have available, since they effectively deny students instruction. Given

---

3 R. Skiba and D. Losen, "From Reaction to Prevention: Turning the Page on School Discipline," *American Educator, 39* (4), 2015, 4–46.

4 American Academy of Pediatrics, "Policy Statement: Out-of-School Suspension and Expulsion," *Council on School Health*, 131 (3), 2013, e1000-e1007.

the natural consequences of missing instruction, it is troubling to know that millions of students from kindergarten through the twelfth grade are suspended each year.

We Have to Want Kids in School

As I briefly described in the introduction, I vividly remember a conversation with a parent after a discipline issue in which the child did something egregious and our response was a suspension from school. We were standing in my office, and I was sharing the disciplinary consequences. Then, the mother stopped me with her hand up, looked me directly in the eyes, and said, "You always say that you are about all kids and will do anything for them. Right? That's your thing. Well, my kid right here needs you now, but you are pushing him away. What are you going to do to help *my* child?"

I have never forgotten how I felt in that moment. She was right. I had the authority to decide exactly how we were going to deal with it. Whether I realized it or not, I did have a choice, and I was letting that student down. How can I tell families that I want their child in school every day and I'm there for them no matter what, but send them away as soon as they do something wrong? It sends a message I can't live with anymore. If I'm all in for all my students, I have to be there for them through the good and the bad.

This is where you separate yourself as a classroom or school leader. Our legacy is defined by how we support our most struggling students. We cannot advocate for our school, sell it to parents, tell students that we want them there, and then kick them out as soon as they misbehave.

I'm not going to be all about kids only when it's easy, only for kids who are nice, or only for kids who look like me. We have to be all in, all the time, for all kids, especially when they make mistakes. We have to be honest with ourselves in education and reflect on what we can do to be better before someone does it for us. Dig deep and challenge yourself to eliminate, not reduce, discipline disparities.

Being students' number one advocate is not going to be easy. You should be the one—if no one else—who has their back when times get tough, because that's when they need you the most. Don't just talk about it; be about it!

CONSIDERING CONSEQUENCES

I know. It's easy for me to say all of this, but what happens when we get into really tough behaviors—the kind that totally disrupt classrooms? If we lower our overall expectations of behavior and just allow misconduct, things will only get worse. So where do we put our energy? Teachers deserve consistency and to understand how their school's discipline procedures work, but automatic consequences are not effective because they don't take in the context and complexity of the situation.

Discipline must be individualized for each student to have the greatest impact. Our students are people, not problems! We must take the time to value each one of them as individuals with hopes and dreams, even if they are disrespectful, disruptive, and defiant. We cannot let their actions and attitudes affect ours. We are professionals and must act in ways that will be effective, not in ways that we think the kids deserve or asked for.

One thing to really watch out for is the automatic consequences that may be built into your school's or school district's policies or regulations. Take a moment to read through them and see how misconduct and consequence are so directly automatic. Then dig deeper. Who wrote the policy? Did it involve a diverse group of stakeholders? Involve students? When was it last reviewed and updated? Modern discipline is much different, and our policies should reflect the changes.

EFFECTIVE INSTEAD OF EFFICIENT

I was sitting with a student in my office one day, and I had a little bit of an epiphany. I was completely overwhelmed, and dealing with a serious discipline problem was not what I needed in that moment. But as I was sitting there, multitasking and trying to answer emails as a student was explaining his home life to me, something made me stop.

I began to listen more carefully, and I couldn't believe some of the things I was hearing. I turned my chair to face the student and completely focused on him in the moment. I *listened*. And listened. And listened. The more I heard, the more empathy grew in my heart. The student in front of me became less of a distraction and more of a challenge. All of the "really important" administrative tasks that were on my to-do list suddenly felt very small.

Sitting there, trying to help this child deal with his trauma and abuse, was exactly where I was needed and where I was meant to be. This was my calling. The student in front of me mattered more than anything else I could possibly be doing. His story changed how I viewed him forever, and the empathy I developed changed how I disciplined him going forward. When you listen to your students' stories, you learn why they act the way they do. They become less of a mystery. "Zero tolerance" suddenly seems intolerable. Student behaviors start to make sense, and the next steps in dealing with their emotions and behaviors start to naturally take shape.

Live in the moment. Stop what you are doing. Listen to their stories and learn from their pasts. When you talk with students, talk with them on their level, not yours. They are not adults. They are children. Even in their teen years, they are still not fully developed and need you to talk at their level—not talking down to them, but at the appropriate developmental level.

When you are disciplining a student, realize that it is the most important thing you could be doing at that moment. Discipline is not something we do as a side thing or that we should delegate to someone else. Take the time that's needed to resolve the issue and deal with it effectively. Multitasking or hurrying through a process only stresses everyone out, including ourselves.

When you are considering what kind of process to use, be careful not to confuse efficiency and effectiveness. Sure, we can quickly run through students, having quick meetings, and check them off our list, but is that really faster in the long run if the behaviors continue? I remember making this mistake as an assistant principal. I thought I was so efficient. I lined up about ten students in the office for all the bus referrals I received. One by one, I pulled them in, gave them the same stern lecture and discipline referral, and sent them on their way. Looking back, while it was fast, it was also overtly authoritarian. I didn't learn more about what was happening, why it was happening, or any potential deeper issues. Context, history, severity, relationship to the student, and other factors are critical to understand before any type of decision is made to redirect the misconduct.

It's all about having a good process. Effective may be slower, but being methodical, analytical, and patient will make all the difference in the outcomes.

STUDENT DISCIPLINE EIGHT-STEP PROCESS

Context matters. That's why I can't advocate enough to NOT create a list of automatic consequences for behaviors. Each situation is unique, and students deserve the right to an investigation and to have their side of things heard. We must avoid a fear-based response to all situations and allow a sense of proportion to predominate. This can be done through differentiating the discipline outcomes based on the context of the misconduct.

Perception matters. We want to show our students and families that we are fair and open-minded, so our practices should reflect that. Define your process for investigations to ensure an unbiased, consistent, and fair approach to considering next steps for a report of misbehavior that warrants administrative action. When you see misbehavior or when others bring accusations to you, consider these eight steps to ensure a fair disciplinary process for all involved.

1. Learn

Investigate the situation with an open mind and learn all viewpoints before making decisions. Slow down and learn the facts first.

2. Listen to Teachers

Talk with staff who witnessed the incident or to whom the accusation was reported in the first place. Be an active listener and write down details and facts, not feelings.

3. Talk to Students

Talk to all students involved individually and help them understand that you are just getting the facts straight and listening at this point. Talking to students individually helps give a stronger sense that you care about student's individual viewpoints.

4. Communicate with Parents

If this is an issue that goes to the office or counselor, talk to all the parents of every student you talked to. Every one. Every time. I know it can feel like a lot, but the investment is always worth it, and the parents may have additional insight or information for you.

5. Get into Detail

Articulate the exact behavioral concern on the table. Don't be vague about this. What was specifically done to cause harm or violate the code of conduct? What was the exact thing that the child did that was wrong, and how would you justify any disciplinary action needed?

6. Review

Review the accused student's past behaviors, potential disabilities, communication concerns, or previous incidents of misbehavior. Don't assume. Look up the facts. Sometimes we have a certain bias toward students based on their race, their gender, what they wear, or what we've heard about them.

7. Decide

Determine if the misbehavior was a disciplinary infraction or if it was an inappropriate behavior. There is a difference. You may find out that the situation was not misbehavior at all. Once you dig into the details, you may find out that it was the accuser who really misbehaved or was not accurate with their story. Make decisions for actions based on what will best improve the misbehavior.

8. Follow Through

Talk again briefly to accused and accusers. Your investigation needs to be accurate, detailed, and factual if you are taking discipline to a more serious level. Be ready in advance with what you are going to say to families.

YOU HAVE THE POWER

Discipline is confusing, but it's not as subjective as it seems. There is a right and a wrong way to do things. School discipline brings stress, difficult situations, and tough choices, and it's draining on all involved. Mistakes happen when we let our emotions get the better of us.

Taking time away from the problem at hand and coming back to it later can give you a different perspective or a much-needed break that allows you to think more clearly. But at the end of the day, realize how much power you have in these situations. We can support the child and redirect the behaviors, but we're going to have think beyond the traditional practices we have used in the past or experienced growing up.

Systems and clear procedures reduce anxiety and bias, and they increase the feeling of fairness, something essential for discipline to be effective. But that doesn't mean that we give up our power to the form or the process. The paperwork is not the point. The form doesn't matter. The child matters. Make up your own mind. It's important not to allow accusers to make the decisions on discipline for you. If there was a clear violation of the code of conduct, review the severity of this issue and its frequency in the past with this student. When you determine what consequence you may or may not give, remember that even just pulling the student from class and reprimanding them is still a consequence. Sometimes that's all they need.

Safety must always be the priority, both for students and staff, and as students age, their misbehavior has the potential to get even more physical and dangerous. As the danger factor increases, so must our sense of urgency and intensity in supports and interventions.

What the hard-nosed approach that we saw in the eighties movies didn't tell us was that exclusion, shame, and punishment can create a self-fulfilling prophecy in our students. Using these strategies will only give us more of what we don't want. Even if others are pushing us toward these traditional practices, are we going to let them make decisions for us that aren't supported by research?

We *can* have both well-disciplined classrooms and a positive and engaging school environment. Our reactions must be tempered with the goals we have for our students and the behaviors we want to see in our students. Think about what *actually works* to get us what we *ultimately want*. When students push away, we need to pull them in. We need them to understand that no matter what they do, we will not turn our backs on them. That is fundamental for building their trust so they begin to look inward at changing themselves.

TIME-OUT

> What is one disciplinary practice that you have seen or one you have used that you know just doesn't work?

> We are driven by our past successes. When have you been the one person to help a child be successful when others had given up on him or her?

> Do you have a clear process in your classroom or in your school to remind you to slow down and investigate each situation?

> What are some ways you can reduce bias and improve relationships throughout the disciplinary process?

CHAPTER 4

UNDERSTAND ROOT CAUSES AND HOW THEY AFFECT BEHAVIOR

WHAT SCREWS US UP MOST IN LIFE IS THE PICTURE IN OUR HEAD OF HOW IT'S SUPPOSED TO BE.—UNKNOWN

How do you handle it when *parents* don't follow instructions?

I used to feel anxious and frustrated when we would have a play, awards ceremony, or other schoolwide function. Parents would cheer when you asked them not to. They would walk to the front to take pictures instead of staying in their seats. They would do so much that was against the rules and almost seemed to push against authority.

But when I considered what to do about it, it was tough to know exactly what would work without having parents become even more defiant or angry at me. Finally, it dawned on me that what they were doing as parents was totally natural and predictable. What if instead of pushing against them, I let go and addressed the root causes of why they were acting that way? In this case, they were overwhelmingly proud of their kids and wanted the moment to be really special for them. Instead of fighting it, I began embracing it. How could I help provide for this need during our time together? I changed. My routine changed. The relationships improved. Now, I ask them at the beginning of an event to all come up to the front and take picture. I make it a big deal. I not only allow cheering, I join in. I've found that by allowing and even promoting these things, parents are provided with what they need, and then they follow the other rules and directions even more. Instead of fighting behaviors that stem from basic human nature, embrace them, use them, and set aside time for them.

In many cases, we ask more of students than we would ever expect of adults in the same context. How many adults are expected to always sit still, never speak out of turn, and always get along with others?

How would we do as adults with the same expectations we put on our students? Look around at staff meetings, team meetings, or parties with friends. Adults can do silly and inappropriate things. Just like adults, students also do silly and inappropriate things at times. These actions are not always misbehavior as much as they are human nature. Just like when I changed my process and attitude on letting parents come up and take pictures, we can also be happier and more effective if we understand and embrace the natural actions of our students.

> **INSTEAD OF FIGHTING BEHAVIORS THAT STEM FROM BASIC HUMAN NATURE, EMBRACE THEM, USE THEM, AND SET ASIDE TIME FOR THEM.**

MASTER OF YOUR OWN DOMAIN

There are many different ways to address typical human behaviors. Companies have intentionally studied human nature to manipulate people into buying things in their stores. Retail business models have evolved with the understanding that knowing the customer and their tendencies can help manipulate how they feel and act in their stores. For instance, changing the tempo of background music can make you shop slower in stores or eat faster in restaurants. The colors in signs can trigger caution (red), increase your appetite (yellow), or make the store feel more trustworthy (blue). Salespeople "mirror," or subtly copy, the gestures and tone of the customer to make the customer pay more attention to suggestions and feel more comfortable. The layout of a store is designed to keep you shopping as long as possible. Comfort levels, aisle width, and product placement are examples of strategies used to make you buy more products.

Stores don't look like they did fifty years ago, but classroom design can often be very similar to how it was back then. While we don't want to actively manipulate our students, we do want to learn about our students' natural tendencies and behavioral patterns. We can use this information to create new systems, new routines, and new strategies.

Do your students tend to always want to exit class in a way that is totally opposite of what you want them to do? Instead of forcing them to do something that is uncomfortable, how can you work with their habits? If all they want to do is talk and socialize as they walk out, and it becomes just too much, be careful to not go overboard with enforcing silence. Capitalize on what you know about your students and create a routine that provides purposeful dialogue between the students as they leave—a dialogue that you choose and control.

We all work hard on classroom layout, organization, and setup, but we usually do so independently from each other. We pick themes and decorations based on *our* preferences and what makes *us* comfortable, but we aren't always thinking about how we can employ these choices as tools to work with student behavior. Do your grade level or department meetings include discussions on this? Take a walk. As a team, tour your rooms together. Share how and why you decorated and organized your materials the way you did. I think you'll find some interesting tips that you may not have considered before.

ALIGNING NEEDS AND SETTING

When we consider what we can control around us, we are empowered to take back command of our classrooms. We have enormous power and control in the school setting.

One of the best benefits of being an administrator is observing amazing teachers in a setting that they created. What I've noticed almost more than anything is that great teachers have so many successful but different ways of running their classrooms. Observe these teachers and you'll see. Ask them, and they'll tell you, like Lisa Keen, a twenty-nine-year veteran art teacher, known for her excellent classroom management, who shares these tips:

> Classrooms should be inviting, but be careful to not spend hours obsessing over decorations that can end up just being more distracting than helpful to students. Extra materials can get in the way of a proper traffic flow in the classroom.
>
> Think about how students will move around your classroom during lessons, for arrival, and for dismissal. Uses stickers, signs, diagrams, and routines to help teach and remind them of the procedures you want them to use.
>
> Clearly outline the materials students need throughout the lesson and have them organized in a way that students can obtain and use them with as little conflict as possible.
>
> Keep your eyes and ears open to see *why* students may be doing what they are doing. Be open minded and

open hearted, and do not automatically blame students or get frustrated.

ROOT-CAUSE ANALYSIS

Sometimes we need to understand what's really happening with a student's behavior to know what to do as educators. Root-Cause Analysis helps us find the real reasons (the *why*) of the behavior we are seeing occur (the *what*), and it should be a go-to method when you have a problem in your class or in your school.

There are many examples of processes to analyze root causes such as five-whys analysis, a fish-bone diagram, and Pareto analysis. Processes are essential to help us step outside of a problem for a little while and look at a situation as analytically and objectively as possible. By targeting the root cause, we can potentially eliminate a condition altogether and prevent the behavior from occurring again in the future.

Makes sense, right? Watch out, though, there are some ways that we can trip up during this process! We are sometimes too vague or broad in describing the behavior of concern. Or we lack input from key participants whose perspectives are needed. Or we too quickly focus on solutions before the problem is fully analyzed. Finally, we may only consider one root cause, when there may be multiple factors causing the misbehavior.

It really is difficult to be totally objective since we are right in the middle of things and may be emotionally invested. You may even be really frustrated or angry. Procedures are essential in making the discussion more about the problem and not about the people.

Some strategies are more complicated than others, and personal preference comes into play as well. Try different strategies and come back to what works for you and your team.

The Five Whys

The five whys is a simple strategy that can be quick and easy to use. It was first used by Toyota in the 1970s as a way for businesses to improve their efficiency in production. This process involves identifying a behavior of concern (BOC) and then simply and repeatedly asking why. As you consider causal factors or symptoms of the BOC, you can begin to better understand the potential root cause of the behavior.

1. Write out the problem or behavior of concern using chart paper or a shared online document.
2. Ask, "Why are they doing that?" or "Why is this behavior happening?" Write down the answer you come up with.
3. Repeat by asking why the answer to your previous question is occurring. Repeat as many as five or more times, if needed. As you list possible reasons why the behavior is occurring, consider if the reason is *the* root cause of the behavior or just another key factor or variable.

   Problem: Students constantly are calling out in class and interrupting my instruction.

   Why? Because they wanted to answer the question.

   Why? Because they want to get attention from the teacher.

   Why? Because they need praise and validation.

   Why? Because they may have feelings of insecurity.

   Why? Because they have not been successful in the past.

   Possible Root Cause: Students are calling out and interrupting class because they need to prove that they can be successful.

Causal-Factor-Tree Analysis

Let's try another strategy that is a little more complicated but allows for a more in-depth discussion of a variety of causal factors. The five whys is efficient, but not always the most effective in problem solving. It can lead down rabbit holes that can distract from the root cause of the problem. Another strategy is called a causal-factor-tree analysis, which is really just a why tree diagram.

Again, start with a statement of concern. Then ask why this behavior is happening. This time, instead of only having one answer, list all the potential answers in a tree diagram. As you keep asking why for each new statement, you'll start to see some deeper issues at play that you might be able to start addressing through organizational or instructional changes.

1. Write the concerning behavior as one statement.
2. Brainstorm and list all the symptoms of the problem you can think of.
3. Connect possible root causes to the symptoms listed.
4. Again, list and connect additional root causes to the already listed root causes.
5. Stop when you list all of the known root causes. Discuss probable primary root cause.
6. Have others review your diagram to help you identify all root causes.
7. Highlight and then write out a possible primary root cause.

Let's try this with a typical situation and behavior of concern: students are off task and misbehaving while waiting in line before changing class.

When you involve teachers and even students in this conversation, you may find a root cause that you had absolutely no idea was even present.

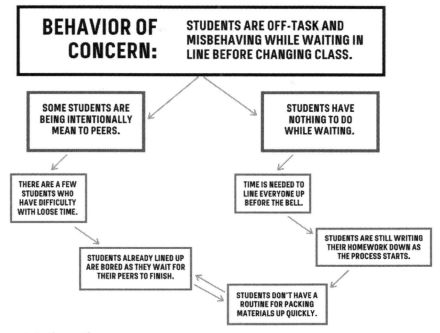

Relations Diagram

One more strategy that creates a more fluid problem-solving analysis is the relations diagram. The relations diagram is another pictorial tool to list out various factors to situations and the relationship they may have not just with the problem, but also with each other. Instead of pure cause and effect, the relations diagram shows how so many factors are related to each other and issues can be very complicated. Factors are connected with lines and the factor with the most connections is typically then identified as the root cause.

Start with the statement of concern. List factors that may cause *or just be associated with the concern*. This can be much more random than the last two examples where items are listed in a more sequential or logical order. In fact, the idea of a relations diagram is to list out anything that could be a factor in the situation and then connect the dots.

1. Write the concerning behavior as one statement.
2. Brainstorm and list all the symptoms, or factors, of the problem you can think of.

3. Connect possible root causes to the factors listed.

4. Instead of adding more factors below each already listed item, this time keep the factors in a large circle as equal players on the field.

5. Stop when you list all of the known factors involved. Connect factors to each other and to the problem of concern using lines. Keep in mind that factors can influence each other and not just one way.

6. The factor with the most outgoing lines will typically be the root cause.

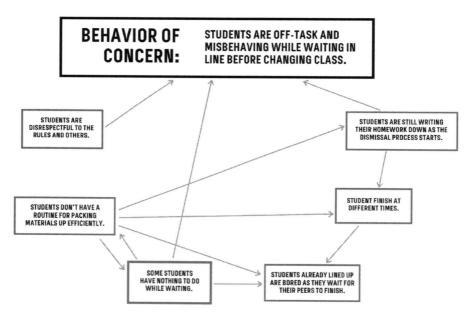

The factor with the most lines leading away from it typically is the root cause. This is not an exact science, but more of a deduction based on context clues. In this scenario, sometimes educators feel like kids are being disrespectful and defiant and thus automatically think that's the main issue to address. Once we dig deeper with a process, we can see that maybe it's really about us having a more efficient process for packing up materials and closing up the lesson instead. Again, we need to be careful to not assign blame to anyone, teacher or student.

Problem solving is about looking at what we can actually do: positive, targeted actions to help make the situation better for all involved.

RESPONDING TO ROOT CAUSES

Just remember that what you find is a *possible* root cause. We may never know *for sure* why kids do what they do. Our job is to learn possible reasons and then help to put plans in place to address these issues. By focusing on one or two things at a time, we maximize our improvement efforts. Addressing the root cause should improve the behavior of concern. There are a few processes that use the primary root cause you've identified in their first steps. It's important to understand these processes, but it's even more helpful to you and the students if you can come up with a plan of action to address the root causes.

If the behavior continues, it may be because you did not identify the true root cause. You may have chosen something important to address, and it may improve things slightly but not fully address the real problem or prevent it from occurring in the future. Help from other stakeholders, especially ones outside of your typical team, can give you additional insight.

If-Then Improvement Statements

One simple way to utilize the root cause you've identified is to turn it into the beginning of an if-then statement.

Write one thing you can do to address the root cause and then write down how you expect it to improve the behavior of concern. If we do X, then Y will happen.

Let's go back to the example situation. Don't forget the root cause we identified: students may be bored while in line, which leads to off-task behaviors.

If we place stickers on the floor leading up to the door, then students will know where to stand and then be in a straight line.

If we reduce the amount of time that students are lined up, then they will have less time to be off task.

If we continue instruction as they line up, such as using exit tickets or lesson summaries, then students will have more reason to be engaged.

Using these if-then statements, we can create a new positive cause and effect that we can control. Take back the power! But don't stop here. Write these statements out in an action plan like the one below.

Place stickers on the floor leading up to the door.

Reduce the amount of time that students are lined up.

Play a video with academic content while they are in line.

Use exit tickets to continue instruction as they line up.

It's critical that you choose a root cause to address that is within your or your team's sphere of influence. That way the action steps you take are actually doable. Keep it small at first with practical solutions that you can implement with minimal resources.

The root-cause analysis process, like any other, takes time. The first time you do it, it will take a little longer than later on when it becomes second nature. Don't be in a hurry. Focus on the process when you are doing it. Go in with positive and constructive intent. Have materials at hand, such as chart paper, sticky notes, and markers. Technological resources, such as online shared boards on Padlet and other shared documents, are great new ways to be really efficient in this process.

BEHAVIORAL GOALS AND IEPS

Students with disabilities are entitled to IEPs that include behavioral goals and instruction if they have a behavioral issue, even if it wasn't part of their original eligibility. That's the law as stated clearly in IDEA: If a student with a disability has an ongoing behavioral concern, they deserve a behavioral goal in their IEP and extra instruction to target that goal.

If you have a child like this now, check their IEP and services for this extra help. Too many kids are disciplined but not provided this mandatory support. Additionally, a functional behavior assessment (FBA) can be conducted, which analyzes the frequency and severity of the behavior and helps find root causes. This is typically followed up by a behavior intervention plan (BIP) to address these root causes and reduce the impact using an official plan of action.

Often, even in our school, we'll realize we don't have an FBA for a kid with serious issues we've been dealing with for a long time. Consult your local district on policies on FBAs and BIPs. Some districts have you sign off for parent permission before conducting these. FBAs and BIPs can be used with all students, not just those that receive special education services.

Even with students that are not in special education, the same actions should be taken. Clear goals that target the root cause of a behavior should be automatic once a student shows a pattern of misbehavior. The faster you address this with a formal plan, the more likely you are to help improve the behaviors. Stop admiring the problem and solve it instead.

I sat down with Laura Ryba, Special Education Teacher of the Year and teacher in one of our autism programs, to get her advice. Here's what she said:

> First and foremost we must know specifically what behavior we are tracking, and we do so by operationally defining the topography (what the behavior looks like) of that

behavior. From there, we can track a student's behavior to understand the trends and patterns. It gives us a good baseline to know the frequency, duration, rate, or whichever measure is specific to that behavior. Once we analyze the data, we can identify the function or reason a behavior is occurring and develop a plan.

Every inappropriate or undesired behavior must be replaced with a more appropriate positive behavior. For example, if a student is making noises in class to gain attention, we must replace that student's behavior with an appropriate response. It is not enough to keep asking the student to stop. In this case it may be appropriate to call on the student when asking questions or have them obtain attention by reading in front of the class. We can also proactively give that student a lot of attention prior to them engaging in that specific behavior to satiate the need. If we do not give the student an appropriate behavior in place of the problem behavior, more than likely, the student will find his/her own replacement, which typically is not a good thing.

Allowing a student to make choices can easily diffuse an unnecessary conflict. While the teacher is in control of those choices, it allows the student to have autonomy and responsibility. The choices students make further connect them to their strengths and interests.

Rewards must be driven by the student. We must align what the student values with the goals set in place. It takes time to intentionally get to know what the student's motivation is and what their long-term goals are. Too often, rewards, such as prizes/tangibles, are put in place that are not really moving the student toward what they value. In creating authentic rewards, we must clarify the goals and help the student identify the behaviors that will move them toward those goals as well as behaviors that could potentially move them away from those goals.

While working to get to know the students in my classroom, I ask each of them what their goals and aspirations are. I have one student in particular who wants to be a YouTuber with a lot of subscribers. With that, I took what this student values to motivate him to reach other goals that would move him to achieve being a YouTuber. I told him that if he wants to get a lot of subscribers he needs to use words that are kind. Each time he uses kind words toward his peers and teachers he earns a YouTube icon.

After a set criteria of icons earned, he gets to (drum roll) make his own YouTube video! This is a clear picture of an authentic reward used to motivate a student by tapping into what they value to meet their goals.

What great advice to help all students, not just those with disabilities. Remember, even the most effective strategies should be specialized to meet the students that need them.

There are many reforms and changes in education that we would love to see, but we can't let the lack of control in those areas affect the things we can make better around us. Be a student of human nature, learning by watching and reflecting on typical behaviors based on age and developmental levels.

There are tangible strategies we can use. We can control a lot in our learning environment. Set up your classrooms and schools to make sense for what your students need to do in each area and throughout the lesson. Know exactly what you want from them and then model it for them every day. Catch their attention, before and as you give them these directions, so you know they are listening to you. If you stop blaming others and make the changes you need to make, you will find that these changes will also make your life easier and save you time in the long run.

TIME-OUT

➤ Choose one of the strategies in this chapter and conduct a root cause analysis on one of the most challenging behaviors. What did you determine as the root cause?

➤ Write an If-Then improvement statement to address the root cause of your problem.

➤ Find out what your students are interested in right now. Is there a way you can connect an experience with an interest to then use an incentive?

CHAPTER 5

TEACH FOR BEHAVIORS WE WANT, NOT THE ONES WE SEE

TOO OFTEN WE FORGET THAT DISCIPLINE REALLY MEANS TO TEACH, NOT TO PUNISH. A DISCIPLE IS A STUDENT, NOT A RECIPIENT OF BEHAVIORAL CONSEQUENCES. —DR. DAN SEIGEL

I happened to walk by a classroom one day and observed a teacher yelling at kids, red in the face, and clearly on the border of out of control. He was angry at the sixth graders in his class for not listening, for constantly sharpening pencils, and for not being prepared or attentive.

This teacher had been using a PowerPoint slide show from a laptop screen at the front of the room. Student were resting their heads on their desks, some with their hoods pulled over them. They continued to get up to sharpen pencils from the pencil sharpener right in front of the teacher, almost as if they were baiting him to get upset. One student was out in the hallway by himself, visibly upset. The kids didn't care about the content, and they didn't care about the teacher. Why should they? It was obvious the teacher didn't care about the students and was running the class with submission and compliance, but somehow he felt that he deserved students who were completely engaged in a lesson that was utterly unengaging.

When I walked into the classroom, it was easy to see how the teacher was quick to look to administration to punish his students. But how can we punish students for behaviors that are a direct result of terrible instruction and behavior by an adult? I don't believe we have a right to do that. There is no way that I could look a child or a parent in the eye and say the misbehavior was the child's fault after seeing that classroom.

We would make a much bigger impact by improving the teacher's skills instead of focusing on the student misconduct. Bad instruction *creates* behavior problems. If the instruction doesn't change, nothing we do with students and their behaviors will make a difference. They will act in typical and predictable ways in response to how they're being treated. Looking inward and reflecting on how we can improve instruction does not mean that we blame ourselves for student behavior. Sure, there are times when teachers should expect bad behavior based on their lesson, but even then, the behavior itself is not the teacher's fault.

We have to stop automatically blaming and instead start doing. Let's work together to improve instruction in ways that will have a positive outcome for behavior without blaming the teacher for their current situation. From my own experiences, both at times feeling blamed and for blaming others, I can see firsthand how damaging the blame game is, for the administrator/teacher relationship, and ultimately for student progress. When administrators create a school culture where teachers *want* to improve their skills because they can see the positive difference they can make, that's exactly what they will do, because they want to, not because they are forced to by others. If teachers feel attacked, blamed, or very often, shamed, then they will just understandably put their walls up and dig in. Most importantly, students need inspired and positive educators in the classroom, so administration has to be better in the exchange of constructive feedback to teachers to not crush them when things don't work out perfectly. So let's talk about what that means, helping teachers understand how to grow a classroom culture where kids *want* to behave.

MANAGER AND LEADER

Teaching is tough, there's no way around it. To be effective in the classroom, teachers need to be both effective managers and inspiring leaders. Throw in a little Harry Potter magic and then you're really on the right track.

Administrators get anxious and sometimes use scripts, tight plans, and micromanagement to control the most difficult situations. Then, when things don't improve, everyone throws their hands up, not knowing why things didn't work. Mistrust of the professional educator in making their own decisions is the disintegration of education. You can't script great teaching and doing so breaks teachers down, not enabling their best selves to develop and learn. Since every group of students is different and every teacher's strengths are unique, there is no script that can cure all of your classroom woes. The best teachers need flexibility to do things *their* way. They need to be able to use *their* talents and strengths in ways that are natural to *them*.

That may sound like a cop-out. But I don't mean that administrators should not provide direction or guidance to teachers. Just like we do for kids, we can scaffold support for teachers in appropriate ways, depending on their skill level. But our go-to strategy to improve behavior cannot always be the latest and greatest scripted intervention.

People say they want exact *steps* to improve things, but mandated instruction can crush creativity. And these *steps* always make more sense to the person that wrote them. Just because they work in one situation, does not mean they will be effective in another. Even worse, teachers can become resentful of these mandates when they don't believe in them or understand why they are needed. We need to think of our work as coaching educators (teachers, assistants, and anyone working directly with students) to grow their skills so that they can make decisions and do their work without your direct oversight. That's the ultimate trust and confidence we should be trying to build. Just like our students, we need to be more patient and think the long game with our staff as well. It takes time to try new things, take risks, and learn what works and doesn't work.

Instead, we need to help teachers understand their roles as effective managers *and* inspiring leaders. We need both, but for different reasons.

We are all going to have different skills and talents that will make us lean more toward manager or toward leader, but *both* skillsets are absolutely needed. Where we should be careful, as administrators, is when we begin to hope that all teachers were one way rather than the other, and our bias would of course want them to be more like us, right? That's called leadership bias. Flip that by instead working to maximize teachers' skills and the personalities they were born with.

Effective Classroom Managers

Effective classroom managers think with their heads. They analyze details in situations, seeking small improvements that can make the biggest impacts. They organize their notes so they can see patterns in progress and adjust instruction accordingly.

Effective managers create new processes and systems in the classroom to naturally improve behaviors. They are prepared with detailed plans to proactively address issues they may expect. They have a keen eye for what's working and not working in any given moment, and are ready to jump in and intervene.

Effective classroom managers can view a behavioral mistake in the context of a child's entire career and not get emotionally caught up in the moment. Because of this, they are able to provide perspective to others and dig down into exactly what next step is needed.

Inspiring Classroom Leaders

Inspiring classroom leaders think with their hearts. They understand that requirements can potentially prevent problems but don't inspire kids to do their best. They look toward the future and potential of every child, aligning talent to praise, seeing the best that the child has to offer. They look for patterns in behavior and find ways to excite the class toward new ideas.

Inspiring classroom leaders use engaging and exciting instruction to hook kids into the learning to reduce boredom and apathy. They are not held back by statistics showing failures. They use their hearts to connect emotionally and raise the expectations of what each child can achieve. Because of this, students are treated without bias and treated fairly, past misconduct is forgiven, and every new day is a new beginning.

Inspiring classroom leaders model tenacity and resiliency. Things in the classroom often go in ways that we can't predict, but these leaders have confidence that we can still get things under control and have a positive impact on our students, no matter what.

PREPARING CLASSROOMS USING FUNCTION AND FEELING

Let's back up and talk about what this means in practical terms. Being both inspiring classroom leaders and effective classroom managers means that we prepare our classrooms using function and feeling, prepare instruction to include behavior and social skills, and finally to never forget the impact that the teacher in the room has on structure, focus, and ultimately student outcomes.

Coming into school and preparing the classroom for students can be a ton of work, but it's also a lot of fun. Teachers pick different themes or organize their spaces in special ways to spice up the year and create excitement. For many it's special seating, fancy bins, colorful posters. For others, their room may be simple and minimal in extra decor. Whoa, right here—time to stop and think:

Who are we actually decorating classrooms for?

I absolutely loved to decorate my classroom. I spent a lot of time trying to get it right. I even put up massive graphics I created on my own with butcher paper and cut-outs. It took me forever, but I loved the final visuals and it helped me *feel* inspired every day. But, if I'm being honest, I think I always decorated and organized the space based on what *I* liked and how it made *me* feel. Since we spend so much time in school, it makes a lot of sense to make our environment comfortable. There's nothing wrong with that. Owning our environment is a critical component to success. Self-efficacy starts with feeling like you can make changes to your immediate situation that will help your life be better.

I've learned so much over the years from decorating and preparing my own classrooms, doing the same with entire schools, and observing many teachers as they prepare. Classroom design is critical in how we prepare for students, but an effective setup can look very different based on the teacher's personality.

Let's consider how effective classroom preparation is built on a foundation of just two things: function and feeling.

Function reminds us to plan learning spaces, pathways, and materials in a way that has purpose, both for instruction and for the needs of our students.

This can be challenging because we don't always know our students or what they need ahead of time. Additionally, each unit or even each lesson may have a different instructional plan that could change the way the students engage with each other and their materials.

Therefore, it's OK and even intentional to leave your room unfinished when students arrive. Help them invest in their space by giving them choice, areas to help organize, and input into the setup. Often, we overlook the obvious—like giving kids more ownership of their learning environment.

Sometimes there are obvious discipline problems that we can fix if we rethink space for function, for example, a student kicking peers' desks while walking back and forth a million times to the pencil sharpener on the other side of the room. Walking around school, I see every single pencil sharpener in the entire school in the exact same location by the door, and then I realize how depersonalized our classrooms really are. Remove the pencil sharpener, not the student!

Function also is about how we pull students into groups, give spaces for calming corners, or transition from one activity to another. Planning out space with function in mind can prevent predictable misconduct.

Feeling reminds us to consider how students connect to the space around them and how it impacts their social and emotional well-being.

Sometimes cutesy rooms work, but sometimes they don't. Sometimes simple and open rooms work, but sometimes they don't. There's more to it than just decoration. Trying to "keep up with the Joneses" on social media can be a time and energy trap if we let it.

Child friendly is one thing, but a classroom stuffed with three-dimensional decorations that absorb every inch of space can feel suffocating for many of our kids, especially ones with sensory struggles. This is another place where can learn from others. Learn from the students themselves by asking them to make inventories of things that make them calm and relaxed. Learn from research about how we can create an atmosphere of calm, tranquility, and reassurance. Students who have chaos in their lives need uncomplicated and peaceful classrooms for learning.

Some teachers do the very bare minimum to their classrooms in preparation. We use the excuses like, "my students don't really want these baby decorations," or, "I share this space with others, so I can't do anything to it." This do-nothing attitude is absolutely not acceptable, no matter the instructional level. The HGTV craze should tell you all you need to know about how important decor and organization is to adults as well as kids.

Why *is* our class environment so fixed? Giving kids more choices about their learning environment makes them feel like the space is theirs.

A professor of mine once started a class in a unique way: he told us to come in but not to sit down. The seats were not arranged yet, and before we did anything, we were going to help decide how to sit together for the class. It was exciting, and we immediately started working with a buzz. We could tell this professor was going to be interesting, and he was. After some conversation as a group, we decided on forming the chairs into one giant circle. It was that spark that worked to form relationships and keep us engaged for the rest of the semester.

This type of engagement needs a plan. You can't wing it effectively, and it won't happen naturally. Placing students in groups without a plan can be dangerous. I remember the many times I would put my students' desks or tables together in groups thinking that this would be the way to automatically create a more collaborative class culture. Soon into the first couple days (or even hours), a child would start to be disruptive within a group, and I'd get stuck in the trap of reprimanding and separating students for misbehavior. It was frustrating, too, since the class design was meant to help with engagement, and it instead led to discipline issues.

Here's the flaw, though: Who *said* the new desk arrangement would lead to engagement? Did I ask the students? Was I helping them figure out how best to learn and how best to collaborate? Do they get to change their class design throughout the day depending on the type of lesson or activity? No, no, and no.

Something to consider is to have students research different designs and come up with their own plans for the learning environment. Provide a few different starter options that you can live with as well. If a lesson's primary activity involves kids collaborating and talking, give them the choice to move all the desks to the side and stand while they work.

Are you already giving these options to your kids now? Take them a step further. Allow students to give input on their voice levels in the classroom, how they transition, and how much direct instruction vs. practice time they get. Don't overlook easy opportunities for changes, such as how they ask to go to the bathroom, sharpen their pencils, or request help. This can be integrated into a lesson by having students research and write up proposals for these changes they want in class. What if the first week of the school year was spent creating these norms together instead of reminding them of consequences or force-feeding academic content?

Classroom decor and organization makes first impressions to students and their families about our instruction. If you really care about kids, you'll put in the extra time to prepare an environment that *inspires* them to want to be there, to feel *comfortable* in the space, and to feel that they have some *control* in how it was designed.

STANDARDS-BASED PLANNING WITH SOCIAL SKILLS IN MIND

Another way to consider preparing for behavioral instruction is to learn from the successes in our academic planning. When students come into school not knowing how to read, our response isn't to blame the students or their parents. Reading instruction is typically positive, fun, and engaging. We don't get mad at kids if they can't read, we *teach* them.

Students are tested as soon as the year begins by the state and by the school to determine their reading level so that we can differentiate instruction and track progress. Teachers plan specific minilessons based on reading objectives and then group students based on levels or appropriate strategies to provide more in-depth and personalized learning experiences designed to improve their reading levels as fast as possible. At the beginning, middle, and end of the year, we track and report these levels to monitor improvement.

For many years, schools have focused on reading levels as an indicator of long-term success for students. The common understanding is that if a child can't read by third grade, they are at a high risk for many concerning outcomes, even including prison time. But do we have the cart before the horse on this? We have spent years highly focused on improving reading, yet we see worse behaviors than ever in schools. We do not have a balanced approach. The increasing focus on standardized academic assessments can even exacerbate behavioral struggles further. Imagine a school that was as targeted and intentional with teaching social skills, self-regulation, and self-discipline as with teaching reading. Let's look at a few ways we can rethink our daily work.

Schedules: Our daily schedule shows our priorities. When a school's typical schedule has mandated blocks of time for math, reading, science, and social studies, you know that academics are clearly the number one priority. Maximizing learning time and eliminating downtime is essential. But do we just teach academic robots, or do we teach human beings with a complex set of emotions and social skills? If we are going to be really serious about adding instruction for improved interpersonal skills, collaboration, or anything along the lines of social-emotional learning, then we need to first create a schedule that has time set aside for this new learning. Integration of SEL into academic lessons is a false promise. Academic content will always be the priority, unless we change the dynamics of how we organize our time. Your schedule is your true reflection of your priorities.

Standards: Schools and districts have extremely detailed academic curriculum and planning documents that they create based on state academic standards. Teachers use these tools to help plan for instructional lessons, focusing on the end goal of learning objectives. Imagine if our behavioral instruction looked the same. I believe it can.

We need to create a set of behavioral standards and then work toward mastery in those skills, in a very similar manner as we do with academic subjects. Lesson plans would be written to align instruction, assessments, and behavioral standards. Teacher teams would gather regularly to unpack the behavioral standards and discuss strategies for instruction. Assessments would target mastery levels of these behavioral skills so we could see exactly what our students knew and could do.

Your lessons should not be random but instead work through a clear progression of skills that build upon each other. What should the student know or be able to do after a lesson? How are they better? How would you know? Creating success criteria that explain exactly how we can know that students have achieved a new skill will help to check mastery. With behaviors or social skills, criteria can be more vague than with academic standards, but the more we treat them similarly, the more we can really track progress toward removing interventions at some point in the future.

A behavior matrix, a grid that lists out desired behaviors for each area of the school, is a great way to create behavioral standards to use for instruction. Don't just make a list of behaviors. Consensus on what are *appropriate* behaviors is critical, or people won't have buy-in to teach them. Come together with a focus group. Use a process. Get feedback from stakeholders. Let your students make changes. Then teach toward your self-developed behavioral standards.

Settings: Do our seating arrangements, learning spaces, and schools in general grant us opportunities for natural social-emotional learning? When every classroom is set up the same, with rows of desks or tables facing the front, it doesn't give us much opportunity to think differently about how we capitalize on social learning. Think of how offices are now created, with hubs and open spaces designed for collaboration and teamwork. Without spaces created for this, it's unlikely to happen naturally. A huge skill to teach students is to understand that they can choose different learning environments for different learning purposes. You might add Starbucks-style seating to promote collaboration but also add individual quiet seating to provide independent work. It may be a little scary to change up our traditional environments, but if we want different outcomes, we have to think and plan our spaces differently. It's hard to work on social-emotional learning and practice social skills while seated in desks in rows. Students need space as well as time to be social. This is something we'll dive deeper into with the next chapter.

THE ANSWER IS LITERALLY ALREADY IN THE ROOM

The teacher is still by far the most important thing in the classroom. Even if you have missteps on the last two pieces, individual teachers can and will make up the difference if they have the right mindset and skillset. These teachers are ones who are masters of their environments, shaping everything around them almost as if by magic. Great teachers make classroom management look easy and it comes so naturally to them, but they are often misunderstood by their colleagues because of this. Setting up students for this kind of success is really hard work and it never ends. It's more than just being tough at the beginning of the year and then coasting the rest of the year. Teachers like this are ones that are constantly scanning, involved, and looking for improvements, even into the last day of the school year.

There are many strategies that great teachers use to help deal with typical areas of misconduct. No one strategy will take care of every situation, and to be a great teacher, you don't need to be perfect. Great teachers do have specific characteristics that make a huge difference with their students' behaviors.

Great teachers are up and out of their seat constantly supporting their students. If you want to have high expectations of your students' behaviors, then you must provide them with high levels of support and structure in class. We need to be present in the moment, not allowing for bullying, teasing, or sarcasm, and having our heads on a swivel, seeing all and knowing all in the room. Teachers need to be active to prevent, catch, and redirect behaviors like these when they occur.

New teachers: please do not be afraid to stop everything in a lesson to redirect students and change things up to get kids back on track. Even if you are being observed by an administrator, it's OK to stop and take back control. It's not a sign of weakness. In fact, it only makes you look stronger and more in tune with what your students need in that moment.

Great teachers constantly reteach their students how to work together. When students break into groups or work with partners, it's not a rush for them to just get started. These teachers understand the opportunity that each of these situations bring to reteach, remind, and review how they should interact. Every time. Over and over again.

As we can see in any reality TV show or see on social media interactions, adults don't know how to work in groups very well, right? They fight, argue, compete, and backstab. Why do we then expect kids to be any different?

Instead of assuming kids will take roles and share responsibility, make it mandatory and establish clearly defined expectations for when people talk, how they talk, and what they say. Use sentence starters and routines. Teach students how to work through problems, how to apologize, and how to accept apologies. Teach and practice how kids should sit, listen to a speaker, and organize their materials. Model all of this yourself and constantly repeat the expectations of not just what students are supposed to do, but how to do it. These basics got lost very quickly in school, with each teacher expecting the previous grade to have mastered it.

Use activities that have natural engagement with talking and doing instead of just sitting and listening. Whoever is doing the talking typically does the learning, so let students talk. If you don't give them opportunities to practice these skills in a safe and constructive manner in class, they will never know how to use them in real life in the hallways or during lunch.

Great teachers are clear with directions. Want a fun activity to try with your colleagues or students to help them understand the importance of explicit and clear directions? Try the "exact instructions challenge" and ask them to write down the exact steps for making a peanut butter and jelly sandwich. Tell them to be as detailed as they can be in each step. Then take their directions and use them to actually make a sandwich in front of them—ONLY doing exactly what the directions state. If the directions are written to spread the peanut butter over the bread, but it doesn't say to use a knife and dip it in the peanut butter first, then show them by taking the entire jar of peanut butter unopened and rubbing it on the loaf of bread!

The more common the expectation is (in this case making a simple PB&J sandwich), the more people tend to assume that everyone around them knows what to do and will do the same way that they do. They call these directions implicit, or implied but not specifically expressed. In the classroom, assumptions like are like ticking time bombs.

Our kids need literal and specific directions for behavior. These directions should be very explicit, stated clearly and in detail. There should be no room for doubt. Unfortunately, many of our directions can be vague and we sometimes leave exact expectations unstated. Don't make success a mystery. Tell students exactly what you want them to do. Model it. Teach it. Review it. Reteach it. We make assumptions about respect or defiance that are rooted in our ability to give effective directions. Explicit and clear directions benefit all students by creating consistency and equity in outcomes regardless of background, language, or ability levels.

Consider again the exact instructions challenge and PB&J. How would students from different countries and cultures do with that activity? Is it fair to assume they know what PB&J is and how to make one? And if they don't know how, is it their fault? There are a ton of other skills they do know that are culturally relevant to how they grew up. Being culturally responsive means to reduce our own bias and assumptions. The practical application is to be very specific with teaching directions and when providing instruction.

Great teachers know what outcomes they want and provide success criteria. Do *you* know what you really want your students to do? Just like in the "exact directions challenge," we sometimes think of the overall task in general and not specific terms. We see most kids knowing how to do something, so we assume that all kids already learned it, should be able to do it, and don't require to be taught again.

Since we have to be very specific when articulating what we want students to do, it helps us to really define what we are looking for in the first place. And in this case, visuals are king and queen of the castle. They rule all other directions. Visuals are more simple and clear than written directions. If you aren't using visuals all over the place, it's something you can do to improve your classrooms right now.

Visuals with step-by-step directions are helpful to model specific expectations for students. Just like detailed plans for making a peanut butter and jelly sandwich, make the directions so clear, in both pictures and writing, that students can't help but follow them correctly. Ask others to review your directions to see how clear they really are to them, not just you. Adding pictures is a big deal. Many of our students have trouble with reading due to a disability or second language. Visuals provide scaffolding and clarity for them.

The most effective strategy for directions is to use pictures of your actual students following the directions. This is more efficient for directions that are used as routines. When you go through the directions the first time, ask students to pause and then photograph each other following the desired procedure. Make sure they are doing it exactly the way you want.

Just by having the task of taking the picture, students will feel that you value them as people and that you are confirming they can actually follow the directions. This strategy is effective in that it allows for and promotes diversity in the models. It is also beneficial because when students see themselves in the models, they are more likely to connect with the steps.

Great teachers value progress as much as overall performance. Students who struggle know that they struggle, right? And they know that they are not meeting the expectations like everyone else. When teachers reinforce students' efforts and progress toward their own individual goals, students will be more engaged in class. When our classrooms become places for all-or-nothing results, kids that struggle will tend to shut down and at times even become distracting to others. Individual goals and benchmarks for success help students to personalize their journey, feel successful even when they are not getting straight A's, and then be more focused on their work.

When students begin to struggle either academically or behaviorally, help them create minibenchmarks for success. Letting them know exactly what they need to do to make progress is the first step to helping them get there. Don't make it a secret. Tell them exactly what they need to do. Keep it small and simple at first.

Students who struggle with behaviors—no matter how awesome we are as teachers—won't just transform into perfectly behaving students at the flip of a switch. It takes time. Things seem to be going well. Then—boom—another major misbehavior and we throw our hands up like nothing is working.

The key is to use data and facts over emotions. Look closer at our student performance over time. Data is powerful. It can show us that even though there is misconduct in the here and now, it might actually be happening with less frequency or having less of an impact over time. That means what you are doing is working! Don't give up! Progress *helps us* stay just as motivated as our students.

WE ALL CAN BE GREAT TEACHERS AND HAVE EXCELLENT CLASSROOM ENVIRONMENTS

Great teaching is tough, but not impossible. And remember, just because you may have classroom issues from time to time, or even right now, doesn't mean you aren't great or that you should give up! Think progress over perfection! Own your situation! Embrace your challenge! Create the change!

TIME-OUT

➤ What is one strength you have as a classroom manager? What is one strength you have as a classroom leader? Which do you feel describes you more, leader or manager?

➤ What if you removed academic pressures to refocus on social-emotional learning today? What would your new daily schedule or lesson plan look like? What stressors would be removed from both you and your students?

CHAPTER 6

CAPITALIZE ON RELATIONSHIPS TO INSPIRE IMPROVEMENT

TRUSTING YOU IS MY DECISION. PROVING ME RIGHT IS YOUR CHOICE.–UNKNOWN

I was working with a student who was constantly disruptive in class. She was disrespectful to the teacher when redirected. She would often get frustrated and distract others when she couldn't do the lesson like her peers.

But when I sat down with her and we spent time one on one, she was like a different child. She was nice, engaged, and didn't display any of the other behaviors that we saw in class. When I asked her about her personal life at home, I realized that her main influence was TV. She had siblings, but they were much older than her, so essentially, she was like an only child. She was left alone a lot at home with a device as a pseudo-babysitter. Her role models were not helping her learn how to behave or act in socially acceptable ways.

I realized why she was so nice with me but a challenge in class. She had no idea how to act in that setting. She was completely overwhelmed with what was happening in the classroom and acted out due to her emotions and frustrations getting the best of her.

I enjoyed working with her one on one, but she was missing essential learning time with her peers whenever we took her out of class. And I'm not talking about the academics. She was missing key social learning time. All these little moments that we take for granted are essential to the growth and development of social skills in our students. Exclusion is a double whammy: it keeps students from getting both the academic *and* the social leaning that they desperately need.

BEHAVIORAL LEARNING THEORIES

There has been tremendous research and even disagreement over the last century on how kids and adults learn and decide how to interact with the world around them. Over time, these changes in learning philosophies mirror the discipline and behavioral responses in education and society.

When I was in my undergrad classes, I thought that hundred-year-old concepts like these were outdated and not relevant for the modern classroom. I was wrong. While there are many critiques and opposing views of the research I've shared in this book, each explains a piece to the complex puzzle of child psychology. Effective teachers and administrators must be part child psychologists. We must understand *why* kids do what they do. This helps us to react more effectively and to predict behaviors. This helps us have patience and understanding for students when they act in ways that are very frustrating to us.

Instead of giving you a detailed dissertation on psychology, let's explore this by describing the experiments these psychologists used and then what they learned or theorized.

Pavlov's Dogs: In 1897, Russian physiologist Ivan Pavlov sought to understand the physiology of dogs from external stimuli. He observed how over time, dogs would be automatically conditioned to understand how a neutral cue (bell) is associated with another action (food). He realized that when a dog heard the bell, it began drooling, which he felt was an automatic and involuntary response. This was one of the early and most famous examples of what is known as *classical conditioning*.

> **Classroom Connection:** Students will automatically begin to associate one thing with another whether we realize it or not. A child may avoid situations that make them uncomfortable or ones they are fearful of. They also will emotionally react to how teachers act in their class. If a teacher is angry or upset, students may then in turn feel sad or anxious. Educators need to be aware of how the various stimuli in school can never be taken for granted. *Everything* affects students one way or another.

The Cat Box: In 1905, American psychologist Edward Thorndike used cats to observe how they learned to interact with the world around them, in his case, a puzzle box. In the box, he included levers that the cat could press to trigger their release to reach a fish they could see outside the box. He learned that the cats' trial-and-error process taught them to escape from the box much faster each time, since they remembered what they learned from their previous time in the box. He suggested a "law of effect" in that learning occurred when actions led to a specific, repeated effect, and is the basis of *operant conditioning*.

> **Classroom Connection:** Students will again automatically begin making connections with the world around them. They learn by observing how their actions have specific effects. We can help them by making this learning process safer and more understanding. When they make behavioral mistakes, it's important to help them learn

from them instead of punishing them. They are experimenting every day in their own lives.

Little Albert Experiment: In 1920, American Psychologist John Watson taught a nine-month-old baby boy to be afraid of things that he wasn't afraid of initially. He let the boy play with a white rat. The boy enjoyed it until Watson started playing very loud and scary noises. His experiment is an example of classical conditioning and would obviously be considered unethical today. He argued that a person's physical response was the only way to see their inner workings and that others could condition people to have outward emotional responses to specific environmental factors.

> **Classroom Connection:** Students learn how to act based on the stimuli they receive in their environment. Additionally, they may have certain behaviors in class that don't make sense to us but exist because of trauma they have grown up with in their home lives or previous educational experiences. This is why school must feel like a calm and safe space for students at all times.

The Skinner Box: In the 1930s, American psychologist B.F. Skinner built on the theories of Thorndike, but this case focused on how rewards were the main driver for the behaviors he observed. In his experiments, he created what would be known as an *operant conditioning chamber* and used a lever for rats, or a key for pigeons, to watch how they interacted to obtain food or water. The food reward was considered a reinforcer of the behavior and thus Skinner could create a behavior desired based on the animal wanting the sought-after food reinforcement.

> **Education Connection:** Educators have the power to control students' actions based on rewards and punishment. That is a serious responsibility and one that should not be treated lightly. This idea of operant conditioning is the

entire basis of many behavioral improvement models and is completely based on our control over students' actions. We shouldn't be treating kids like animals in experiments, waving a discipline referral at them or bribing them with trinkets so they act in ways we want.

Constructivist Experiments: Starting in 1920s, but not becoming more known until the 1960s, French psychologist Jean Piaget began his experiments by observing his own three children and then conducted tests in person with kids in schools. He observed how they developed through different stages over time and that each stage had specific characteristics that we could expect to see in other children at that same stage. Piaget had a constructivist approach, arguing that children constructed skills and knowledge by building upon previous experiences and that older children could help guide younger children since they had already moved on to the next stage of development. He also explained that learning was more about internal cognitive development than the external factors that previous psychologists discussed.

Classroom Connection: Intelligence is not a fixed trait and develops over time as children age and experience life. We have to be careful not to put adult expectations on children and even teenagers. They will act in ways that are developmentally appropriate for their age, and we must have patience as their brains and social-emotional intelligence develop. In academics, we readily accept that students cannot grasp certain math and reading concepts until they get older. We would never punish them for not being able to read as they start kindergarten. Behavior should be considered in the same way. Peer mentors that have learned these behavioral lessons are a great tool to help kids reflect and build new skills upon previous experiences.

The Bobo Doll Experiment: In 1961, Canadian American psychologist Albert Bandura used a plastic, clown-looking inflatable propped up like a punching bag (that I describe it this way gives you insight into my psychology). Bandura used multiple scenarios in which kids observed an adult interacting in positive or negative ways with the Bobo doll. In one scenario, the adult used objects, fists, and angry language to hit and yell at the doll. In another scenario, the adult used trucks, dolls, and other toys to interact in positive ways with the doll. In both scenarios, the students then were sent in to play with the objects in the same room. As you may predict, the kids that watched the negative actions were in turn much more likely to do the same, and vice versa for the separate group of kids that watched the positive adult model. He theorized that people learn through observations of social interactions in others and tend to repeat those same actions, including attitudes and emotions. This is the basis of *social learning theory*.

> **Education Connection:** Educators themselves are behavioral models for their students. Students watch, observe, and imitate the actions they observe in their families, their community, and their school. While we cannot control the actions at home, we can provide an excellent social model for our students while they are with us. We also can help promote and teach positive interactions between peers so they can learn from those experiences.

SELF-EFFICACY

All of these theories on learning are essential to review because they each provide lessons on how students learn how to behave through internal and external factors. No one theory explains everything on how people at and think. Ultimately though, being an experienced educator, I think Bandura's theories connect with me the most. Bandura didn't settle on the idea that students only imitate what they observe, but also that they could make cognitive decisions on whether the actions they observe were in their own best interests or met their goals. Thus, Bandura modified *social learning theory* into *social-cognitive learning theory* in 1986. Over time, psychologists have moved from thinking that only external stimuli totally affected reactions (behavioralists) to realizing the impact of our cognitive ability on the decisions we make about those reactions.

Social-cognitive learning should be foundational to the behavior-improvement strategies we use in school. The practical side of this is to help students develop their own sense of self-efficacy and agency so they can decide whether they should act in ways their peers do or in ways that match their goals in life.

John Hattie, in his research in *Visible Learning*, found that collective efficacy, the ability of a group to be fully confident that it can achieve overall success, has the greatest influence on student achievement. But in order to have *collective* efficacy, we must first have many individuals with *self*-efficacy. Hattie confirmed this by observing that successful classrooms also had individual teachers with self-efficacy (0.75 effect size). But it still goes back to Bandura, who described self-efficacy as the belief we have as individuals that we can reach our goals despite what's happening around us.

Teachers with the most self-efficacy have the best outcomes and the best handle on discipline. But self-efficacy doesn't always look the same in every teacher. Often, teachers with a high sense of self-efficacy are very quiet and humble. There is an inner confidence and strength that is not visible. This self-efficacy is sometimes part of people's personality but only becomes apparent in tough moments—the kind that offer opportunities to grow your inner strength. A major part of self-efficacy comes from knowing that you have been there, done that, and can do it again. This sense of purpose and can-do attitude is contagious to others, just like we've discussed with social learning and conformity theories.

If we want to see our students push through their personal challenges, then we first need to model those behaviors in the classroom.

They are watching everything we do, especially when things get tough. How we react and respond is what they learn. That's why it's so important to be cool, calm, collected, and confident when publicly dealing with issues.

So perhaps we should consider thanking our challenging students. They force us to be better versions of ourselves, to rise up and find solutions to impossible problems. Seeing the whole child in a student who disrupts the classroom is tough; it's also impressive and important. And if you feel like you've failed in a situation, rethink it as a unique gift that will mold you into a stronger person. Each situation provides lessons, even those we perceive as failures. Part of self-efficacy as a teacher is knowing are no real failures in discipline situations except those we don't learn and grow from or the ones where we quit on our students.

We are defined not by our struggles, but how we react to them. We won't be perfect, and we will make mistakes. Our schools and classrooms are defined by how we support our most challenging students and situations. We will have tough moments and face difficult situations.

Social Modeling and Social Persuasion

Because we know that students watch others around them to learn how to act, consider how vital it is for children to have appropriate models around them to learn from each day. And because Bandura's research also explains that children tend to learn more from those that look like them, it's clear that gender and race play a significant role in how kids pick their role models. Schools should be looking to diversify their staffs to reach the wide range of students they serve if they want to maximize their impact as role models.

Students who struggle to behave need positive peer models to show them the way. So when we exclude students, we take away a necessary tool to improve behavior. Social modeling is why it's so important not to exclude students with challenging behaviors, because one of their greatest needs is to have positive peer models around them each day.

You can't model behavior to a student that's not in class because they've been suspended.

We must model the behaviors and attitudes we want to see in our students. We can't fake it. They can always tell if we actually believe something or not. But they also see what we do, how we go about our work, how we organize and complete our tasks, our work ethic, and how we respond to adversity.

Consider the many negative environmental factors that influence our students and the way they behave. It's staggering to hear the movies our students watch and the behaviors they observe in their homes. I remember sitting on the floor with a student in my office who'd had a rough day. His behaviors had really been impacting not only his learning but that of the rest of his class. I knew we couldn't get into changing his behaviors until we could grow our relationship and help regulate his emotions. The first thing I did was just let him talk—whatever he wanted to talk about. And this wasn't because I had a lot of free time. I was really busy that day, but I knew I had to slow down to help gain any little bit of forward momentum. Open-ended, non-academic, non-threatening discussions with kids provide insight into students' personal lives. This student knew all about every scene from the movie *Deadpool*. He thought it was funny and loved the gore. He was seven. Inwardly, I cringed and tried not to reprimand him for his choices, realizing that his life was determined by his parents' choices as much as his. This is what we are dealing with. Kids are watching *Saw*, practicing sniper headshots in *Call of Duty*, and seeing real abuse at home. Negative influences in our students' lives greatly impact their emotions and behaviors. We need to do everything we can to counteract these environmental factors.

Some kids have positive environmental factors and may not need the same level of intensity on our part. Other kids need as much positive and intentional influence in school as possible. Think of it as an intervention. When you have students or even an entire class or school that has these kinds of home influences, focus on creating extremely positive routines each day and throughout the day. This can't be contingent on their behaviors. It can't be used as a reward or positive reinforcement. It has to be given with no expectations on the students. They need as much as they can get. Consider it preemptive discipline.

MASTERY EXPERIENCES

Success breeds success. When students and staff have small wins, they gain momentum and confidence that they can accomplish more. Consequently, many self-help strategies focus on small wins before big wins. These strategies advise us to think small at first, aiming for manageable small, quick wins that help us gain momentum. We can't focus on big wins at first. Those take time, and it's more effective to build upon smaller victories.

As educators, we can provide small wins for our students each day to help motivate them and keep them with us on the journey for self-improvement. This is the basis of positive-reinforcement systems. The more our kids struggle, the smaller the wins need to be. Praise them for everything they do. Be grateful for everything they do. Even something as basic as just them walking appropriately through the door should be recognized and appreciated.

USING SOCIAL LEARNING TO
DRIVE IMPROVEMENTS

Let's review a couple of classroom scenarios. Each of these events happened to me when I was a student. I still clearly remember the experiences, both what I did wrong and what the teacher did in reaction to my bad behavior.

(1) A teacher was seated grading papers at the end of class. A student, visibly frustrated, comes up to argue a bad grade on a group project. Not looking up from the

other papers, the teacher tells the student that the grade was finalized and there is nothing that can be done. The student storms off, muttering swear words at the teacher. What would you do?

The reason I stormed off in a huff and puff was the lack of attention or even care that the teacher showed me. It really wasn't about the grade, something that obviously didn't matter in the long run. It was about the lack of respect.

What did the teacher do? Wrote me up on a discipline referral and gave me detention. The teacher never established a positive relationship, and we battled for the rest of the course.

(2) A teacher hears an argument brewing between two students that quickly escalates to shouting. Looking up from their desk, the teacher sees a young man shove his books and papers onto the floor and storm out of the class. What would you do?

The reason I stormed out of class had nothing to do with the lesson or with the teacher. I was frustrated with many other things going on in my personal life at the time, the feeling that I lacked control and the overwhelming nature of the conflict I was in during that moment. When students storm out of class, it's often because they know they are about to emotionally explode.

What did the teacher do? Chased me down the hallway. But just as I thought I was going to get another referral, I instead received an arm around my shoulder and a question about whether I was OK. As I started to melt down with the teacher, a new relationship was established, one that helped me act better in the class for the rest of the year.

(3) A teacher sees a student struggling to focus in class and engaging in many off-task behaviors. Knowing the potential of the student, the teacher is frustrated. The teacher felt like something needed to be done. What would you do?

The reason I was off task was because I had way too much happening in my life. My family situation at home at the time wasn't good. I was involved in too many school programs, and I didn't have a clear sense of purpose.

What did the teacher do? Asked me to stay after class to chat. Told me that they would be there for me no matter what was going on at home. It wasn't the actions I needed at the time. Just the mere acknowledgment that I was more than just what was seen in class was profound and something I have never forgotten.

I can remember each situation like it was yesterday. I'm not ignorant of my own misbehavior and each time I was in the wrong. But what I really remember is how the different teachers reacted. Reactions that promoted a relationship made all the difference in the world. I didn't deserve second and third chances, but some of my teachers gave them to me anyways. I can't let those opportunities go to waste. Even now. I owe it to *my* teachers to continue that kind of relationship-building with my students. As an adult, I've never forgotten those moments. They are at the core of my discipline philosophy.

ALTERNATIVE DISCIPLINE

A student was brought to my attention one day for being totally off task and unfocused in class which resulted in him being a major distraction to others. It was significant enough that he needed a break from class or things were going to go bad quickly. In a situation like this, many times an administrator would give the student a stern talking-to and send him off back to class. Been there, done that.

Something about the situation gave me pause. It may have been that I didn't want to get back to my emails or the reflection on the many extra chances my own teachers gave me, but I think it was the look of inner turmoil in the boy's face that got my attention and tugged on my heart strings.

"Come with me," I said. "Let's get to work."

I found a bunch of boxes of supplies that need to be delivered to classrooms that teachers had ordered. The student helped me stack them on a cart, and we headed off into the hallway. When we came to the first room, knowing that he was watching, I was very intentional about how I handed over the materials and treated the teacher. As we went room to room, I started having him take over this role. We talked about how to be positive and professional. About how it felt good to help others. By the end, I was impressed with how respectful he was to the staff and how well he followed directions. He was a pleasure to be around. I felt great, too, like I was really making a difference.

When we consider what works and rethink how the future of school discipline can look, we must focus on the power we know social learning and relationships have on changing behaviors. This is the basis of "alternative discipline," a term used to describe the more modern, relationship-driven approach to school discipline.

Alternative discipline is not about just letting kids do what they want. Students need to know what is expected of them and how meeting those expectations will benefit them. Alternative discipline is about being intentional and purposeful in our preparation and then later in our reactions. In almost all cases, when a student has a discipline incident, they are returned to the same school and same classrooms they were in before the incident. How they return and reassimilate into the group is dependent on the student's understanding of what they did wrong and how that affected others. Alternative discipline tends to be based on repairing harm and restoring relationships, both noble goals—but what about kids that don't have any positive relationships to begin with?

I believe that we need to be even more intentional in ensuring that students with misconduct are provided with positive and meaningful relationships with staff and peers. Reframing this helped me consider what really works to change behaviors. It's a culture thing—both in classrooms and in the entire school. Relationships should be at the heart of everything we do in our schools.

Relationships aren't just a part of discipline; they are everything in discipline.

During my dissertation for my doctorate, I studied schools that were able to eliminate suspension for students with disabilities during a two-year period. The school leaders came to one really strong agreement: the main way they were able to do this was by ensuring a positive and

> RELATIONSHIPS AREN'T JUST A PART OF DISCIPLINE; THEY ARE EVERYTHING IN DISCIPLINE.

meaningful relationship between a staff member and every student, especially ones with behavioral challenges. Once they know the student well, then they are able to add personalized supports and accommodations to help them improve. The relationship, though, is key.

When do we know if we have established a positive relationship? There were many times when I interacted with students but didn't really feel connected. Ever feel that way? Sometimes, it's because I didn't invest enough time with them, I wasn't singularly focused on them, or, frankly and honestly, because it wasn't a priority for me at the time. Not proud of that, but it's real. It takes a ton of work to establish and keep a great relationship with a student. You know you are in a great relationship when the student feels that you accept them for who they are, are putting their needs above your own, and ultimately are inspiring them to be the best versions of themselves. Do your students feel that way about you? Do they accept you and want you to be your best version as well? If so, you know you have something special.

Alternative discipline is really about relationship-driven responses to misconduct. The next time you a student comes to you with misconduct, consider the four Rs: relate, reteach, repair, and redesign. As you read through the components of alternative discipline, consider how each could be a theme integrated into everyday life across the school and in classrooms.

Relate

Every student needs meaningful relationships with staff members and their peers. Relating to them where they are will help us with next steps for improvement. It also helps them know they can trust us. Kids change because they want to, not because they have to. Kids change because they care about those asking them to change.

If you want to improve a child, it's about connecting before correcting.

Many of our struggling students have unhealthy relationships with those around them both in school and at home. Unhealthy relationships can make them feel anxious, angry, hurt, or unsure of themselves around others. Negative influences form bad social habits that are hard to unlearn. Those that have unhealthy relationships may not even know how they are being affected by them. They may not know anything else.

Positive relationships in school model and teach healthy relationships through intentional, consistent, and positive social interactions. Healthy relationships have all the benefits that we are looking to provide our students: acceptance, self-control, pruning of bad habits, and increased confidence.

You may not always be the one to relate to a struggling child. If you truly have a school team, then finding the right staff member match for each child is attainable and essential. That's why every staff member should be included as potential student/staff relationship pairings.

Relationship-Driven Interventions

Because these interventions need people and discussions, they need time as well. There are many strategies that schools can and should use to focus on relationships in their interventions.

Check in and check out: Check in and check out typically utilizes a staff member other than the homeroom teacher to have brief individual meetings with a student every day, sometimes twice per day. The focus of the conversation is to find out how the student's day has gone and how they are working toward their goals. Most importantly, this guarantees at least one positive interaction with an adult each day. Find time for the check ins and protect it.

Two by ten: Two by ten is another strategy that focuses on growing relationships. While check ins usually are performed by staff who are not the regular teachers of a student, two by ten is a great way to have even the child's homeroom teacher refocus their efforts to connect. Use at least two minutes of active listening every day for ten consecutive days. Don't talk about the student's grades, their shortcomings, or their goals unless they bring them up. Talk about life. Make a connection. Show that you value them as a person. Watch your relationship change after only ten days.

Take ten: Ten by two goes to another level with the take ten strategy. Instead of only two minutes, find time for ten minutes. If you say you don't have time, consider how interfering the child's behavior is and how much time they are taking away from instruction already. As students' behaviors become more problematic, our intensity and frequency in relational responses must increase.

Preferred activity: Find an activity that the student likes to do. This could be drawing, playing basketball, or playing with LEGOs. As you play together, the student relaxes and begins to open up. Since they are doing a preferred activity, they associate their time with you as fun and enjoyable, and they will even look forward to the "intervention."

Whatever you choose to do, focus on fostering relationships. When students know you care, they care about improving themselves.

The worst thing is apathy, the feeling of hopelessness and despair. The deeper the student is in that hole of despair, the more time and energy you need to spend to build ladders of relationships to get them back out.

Reteach

Every day should include instruction on behavioral conduct. And just because you taught it, doesn't mean they learned it. Some skills need a lot of practice to master. Reteaching (and relearning) includes a reminder and emphasis that behavioral instruction should be integrated into every lesson, every day, and throughout each location in the school. Simply reviewing the rules at the beginning of the year is not enough to ensure that students master behavioral expectations. The old-school idea was that if teachers can be tough during the first few weeks, students will understand the rules and then behave for the rest of the year. That makes teaching sound so easy. We know it's much more challenging and complex than that.

Class Meetings

Class meetings are one way to integrate behavioral reteaching into your day. There are many ways to do class meetings, but a few key ingredients are necessary to make them effective:

1. Help students learn to lead the meetings. Even at a very young age, kids can be very successful with leading.
2. Review behavioral expectations every day for the most common problems you see in class.
3. Build in time for students to greet and talk with teach other to further establish relationships with peers. Routines that break students out of their cliques are sometimes necessary.
4. Allow for students to bring up things that are affecting their learning or success in class and problem solve as a group to fix them.

Teachers who make classroom meetings as important as content instruction will in turn see their academic outcomes improve. The time you spend will be returned double with students feeling more invested in your class and each other.

Buddy Classes

At the elementary level, many schools have a buddy reading program where classes are paired up for older students to help read to and with younger classmates. For instance, a fifth-grade class may meet weekly with a second-grade class, and each student would have their buddy reader to look forward to meeting with. Not only does this obviously build relationships across the school, there is a potential behavioral instructional opportunity with buddy classes.

Buddy behavioral programs build upon the research of social learning (Bandura) and constructivist learning (Piaget). Older students recently have learned lessons that they can teach to the younger students. We can focus on specific topics to review as a class and/or give time for them to talk things though student-to-student.

A possible lesson could look like this: Read a social-emotional focused picture book. Then have students discuss and react to a specific prompt you provide. Students journal out their reactions and reflections on what this means for how they and peers should interact with others.

Buddy classes shouldn't be reserved for just elementary age. Consider the positive impact that high school seniors can have on freshmen, or eighth graders with sixth graders. The trick is to plan it out thoroughly to ensure it stays positive and productive.

Direct Instruction

What if we planned and instructed students how to behave and socially interact with others in the same way we planned and instructed academics? This would include direct instruction using minilessons, anchor charts, and guided practice. While you may not be able to add a specific course like Behavior 101 into your school day, you can throw in quick lessons to reteach desired behaviors based on misconduct you may be seeing in your class. A few examples include:

- A student-created PowerPoint presentation explaining recess rules and expectation using kid-friendly language and visuals. Students could present to peers or even just to the teacher.
- A student-led discussion using a T-chart of appropriate and inappropriate student behaviors when eating lunch in the cafeteria. Students could then describe the ideally behaved cafeteria student.
- A thinking map drawn out by students on of ways they have described that they can get off task in class. Students can offer modifications of lessons, the classroom environment and suggest what the teacher can do to help them get back on track.

Reteaching can range from simple reminders and redirection to creative personalized projects. The trick is to stay focused on helping the student learn what should be done instead of problem behaviors.

Repair

Every time we work with major misconduct, we need to bring more awareness about the larger situation to the student who was acting out. How did it affect their own learning and the learning of others? Why were others so upset? Don't assume they know the answers to these questions. We need to help them reflect and review the factors led to their decisions for misconduct and the consequences of it. This might appear simple on the face of things, but like many of the practices in this book, if used incorrectly, it can circle right back to traditional discipline.

When students are told to reflect on their behavior, they are typically asked to write down what they could do better in the same situation if it were to occur again. They may also role play the situation or take time to discuss it with a staff member. There is a time and place for individual reflection, but I argue that it is not as effective without a trained staff member or someone the student already has a positive relationship with participating. When it comes to minor misbehaviors, teachers are good at talking with students and helping them understand what they did wrong, especially for issues the student may not have realized were a big deal or even considered misbehavior. For this to work well, the teacher must go into the conversation with patience. Doing the typical process—griping at a student about what they did, lecturing them on how they should have known better, and then telling them to go sit in the corner and write down what they did wrong—just won't be very effective. A teacher can be much more effective in helping students reflect if they can do the following:

1. Sit with the student at their level, away from other students. Always take if off the stage. Ensuring we keep private conversations private is essential and builds trust.
2. Listen patiently and in a nonjudgmental manner as the student describes their perspective on the situation.
3. Help the student identify how their misconduct affected their own learning and the learning of others.
4. Brainstorm ways for the student to think about what they could have done differently to get different results. Write these down and come up with a plan for next steps.

The teacher's knowledge of the student will offer insight into the type of reflective exercise that is needed at the time. For example, if the student has difficulty in writing, the teacher might choose to write the words down for the student.

Here are three questions you can use when communicating with students after a disruption:

- Your side of the story is important to me. What happened from your point of view?

- This seems like a tough situation you were in. How did this affect your learning and the learning of others?
- I know you didn't mean to cause harm. What do you think are some ways we can resolve this next time?

By validating their opinions on the situation, you lower their defenses. By taking time to sit with them, you grow the relationship. By asking open-ended questions, you allow them to be open and honest. By focusing on learning, you get away from the power struggle of compliance.

RESTORATIVE DISCIPLINE

Restorative discipline is an increasingly popular approach to improving a school's behavioral climate and addressing misconduct through conflict resolution and repairing harm. These practices teach kids that they can make mistakes but also that they do can harm to others when that happens. It also teaches kids how they can make amends. Restorative discipline means restoring relationships and restoring a calm and productive feeling in the classroom and school. Sometimes this happens in a brief meeting between students, but many times it is more intense and structured. A key ingredient is for the student who engaged in misconduct to realize what harm they did to others and then make some type of restitution using a system like the following:

1. Give everyone a voice.
2. Actively listen and validate concerns.
3. Determine next steps based on what is in the best interest of everyone involved.

Restorative discipline requires thinking and planning. One challenge is that it takes a lot of patience and judgment to determine the right course of action. It is not as simple as just looking at a form and seeing that if a student did X, then they are disciplined with Y. Another challenge is that it is more effective if the student who engaged in the misconduct agrees to the restitution. When students are totally non-compliant with even the later stages of restitution, staff can get stuck on what to do next.

The best way to combat these challenges is to help the student realize that restorative responses are in their self-interest. Praise them and recognize them for efforts to restore relationships with their peers. Work with them to find ways to provide restitution. Restitution is tricky and needs to be carefully considered. It also doesn't always have to directly involve the victim, and sometimes it's best if they are not involved. Here are just a few simple examples of restitution to help you think about this:

- An apology note to a teacher for disrupting class listing three ways the student will improve their behavior.
- Helping a peer redo an assignment or project that they interfered with.
- Creating care packages for families in need after teasing or bullying peers.
- Checking, cleaning, and organizing the computer lab for a period of time after using technology in the lab inappropriately.

Restorative circles are a common way to integrate restorative practices into a school. When students have interpersonal conflicts with peers or staff, consider using restorative circles to resolve the issue. With this strategy, students and teachers each have time to talk about their concerns, the harm they caused or received, and ways to make reparations for the damage done.

Restorative practices go all in on growing and maintaining relationships between students and between students and teachers. Repairing harm may lead to other types of responses like reflection or reteaching. It helps if a culture of understanding already exists in the school, with staff aware that automatic consequences will not automatically change behavior. When staff members understand that the restorative circles and practices are also in their best interest, they will be more likely to buy in and use them. We can model this by using restorative circles ourselves as a staff where there is conflict or a problem arises.

No individual school, principal, teacher, or even "expert" will know how to do all of these strategies, so we need to make sure we keep the collective in mind and continue to learn from others. I asked my friend Brad Weinstein, coauthor of *Hacking School Discipline* and former school leader, to share his experience and explanation of restorative practices:

> The mindset of the adults in the building is the very first item that must be addressed when building a restorative culture in a school. Many educators did not experience a restorative environment as students themselves and before, during, and after becoming educators, many were taught classroom-management strategies that focused on compliance over connection. Some educators can focus on how to "fix" kids in order to get them to do what educators want them to do. The reality is that compliance doesn't address the root cause of behaviors, it doesn't build social-emotional capacity where there might be gaps, and it doesn't address the fact that some kids do not feel connected to teachers or the other students in the classroom. Worse yet, compliance without connection can harm our most marginalized student populations the most. Unconscious bias, a lack of culturally responsive practices, and other factors can add to the disproportionality in discipline that can be seen in many schools around the world.
>
> We must dispel the myth that there are no consequences in a restorative approach, so that educators understand the benefits of making a change. I would argue that restorative practices hold students more accountable than traditional practices, just in a different way. Owning behaviors and repairing the harm through logical and restorative consequences does not allow students an easy

way out where they simply serve time in detention, or are suspended or expelled.

While punitive measures do hold students accountable, it teaches them nothing except that there are consequences to actions. It does not address the needs of not only the student who caused the harm, but the others that are harmed by their actions. It is sometimes easy to defend practices that are comfortable and that are seemingly working within the walls of a classroom or school, but schools should dig deeper and reflect on how effective these are with *all* of the students in the school.

When working with adults, it is important to start small through building awareness of the differences between traditional discipline and a restorative approach. It is also helpful to share and dissect discipline data as it often shows that our students with an IEP or our traditionally marginalized students are often at the receiving end of more referrals, suspensions, and expulsions. If educators are not aware of this, especially with the students in their building, they might not understand the sense of urgency to act in order to mitigate the disproportionality. When I say "act," I don't mean a quick fix but rather taking a restorative approach to relationships and discipline that is developed over time. They must develop a restorative mindset and the skills that it takes to be effective with students.

One recommendation for getting started is to do an optional book study with staff to build capacity with those that are interested in the practices. It is beneficial to start with a core group that can try the practices, fail at the practices, and keep iterating along the way. These educators can be the champions of change and help inspire others to join them. Trying a few things slowly without top-down directives reduces anxiety and builds intrinsic motivation. If an entire staff is forced to do an initiative, there will be push back from some staff members and the practices will either be done out of compliance or ignored completely. Once staff in the building have successes with the practices, it is much easier to spread them, because they are being done with real educators with real students in your building.

It's important to utilize the help of experts in the field, as restorative practices or any approach to discipline, if not executed well, may actually cause more harm than good. It is also beneficial to reach out to other schools that are currently using these methods so that you can identify what is going well, learn what they are currently refining, and talk through the pitfalls that they've experienced so that you do not make some of the same mistakes. The change process takes time, it takes patience, it takes support, and it takes courage, but it is well worth the journey.

Brad has such great advice for schools and teachers to take next steps with restorative practices. Let's think more strategically in our implementation of something as mind-shifting and innovative.

TRUST

Remember that we must be excellent models for the actions we wish to see in our students. We tell them that if they trust us, follow us, and listen to us, we will help them pass tests, have friends, and feel confident in school. But trust has to be earned, and that starts with how you carry yourself personally, how we work together as a team, how you model the work that needs to be done for them, and how much they know that you will be there for them no matter how difficult things get.

TIME-OUT

> Which of the learning theories did you already know? Which did you not know? How do they relate to your day-to-day work?

> Describe a time that you were challenged with really hard work or a tough situation and you pushed through. What made the difference for you?

> How do you ensure a positive relationship with every child in your class or in your school?

> Recall an experience where the relationship with a student made all the difference in the world to their progress. Share this story with a colleague and reflect on why the relationship was so special.

CHAPTER 7

SHIFT FROM EXTERNAL REWARDS TO SELF-REGULATION

WHEN OUR LITTLE PEOPLE ARE OVERWHELMED BY BIG EMOTIONS, IT'S OUR JOB TO SHARE OUR CALM, NOT JOIN THEIR CHAOS.—L. R. KNOT

I had a student dropping f-bombs on me one day and telling me how much he hated me. We hadn't even made it to Wednesday of the week yet. Good times, right?

He was visibly upset and trying to dominate the situation and push me away physically and emotionally. I knew this student. I knew the situation, the triggers, the needs. It was easy to get caught in the power struggle, but instead my reaction was pretty matter of fact. I leaned toward him and said calmly, "This isn't the first time someone has said this to me, and it probably won't be the last time. But I'm not going anywhere. I'm here for you no matter what you do or say." And then I sat back and just waited patiently. Sometimes we just need to quietly out-stubborn our students, but with patience and love.

Before we help our students, we need to check ourselves—even better, know ourselves. Our physical and mental health must be optimal before we start helping others. If we are anxious and overwhelmed, we are not able to be of value to students and might even make a situation worse. That means that when our students bring their heightened emotions and turmoil to us, we must separate what they are dealing with from our own well-being.

Our students are dealing with trauma from society, from their families, and from their personal lives. The invisible weight of this trauma often trips them up on small cracks in their path. Sometimes, an issue might seem small to us—like a child not being allowed to be first in line—but even in seemingly minor situations, consider that a child's feelings and opinions are just as valuable as yours. Even if we know better from experience, our job is not to crush students' emotions into submission but to help them understand the world around them and their place in it.

We all love to watch celebrities fighting on TV, knights in armor fighting dragons, and other really intense and exiting moments in our favorite shows. We have to be careful not to bring in that same kind of drama with us to school. In fact, our role as professionals is the opposite: to do everything within our power to minimize conflict and stress for our students.

LOCUS OF CONTROL

Students who struggle view themselves as failures. They have already lost hope. They often feel like they might as well be what everyone already thinks they are. Students who have problems *know they have problems*. They live these problems *every day* and *every night*. Every time they screw up, their teachers remind them of their problems.

They go home and their parents yell at them about their problems. How do we stop this vicious cycle and often self-fulfilling prophecy?

When we are trying to help our students with these feelings, it helps to think of a concept called *locus of control*. First described by Julian Rotter in the 1950s, locus of control explains the degree to which we believe that we have influence and even control in the outcomes of our lives.

When we feel that our own choices and efforts dictate events in our lives, our *internal* locus of control increases. With this increase comes many psychological benefits, such as greater happiness, better health, and the ability to cope with adversity. When kids struggle, it is often due to environmental factors outside of their control, and they may develop a strong *external* locus of control. This makes them give up on trying harder to make improvement, since it seems that nothing they do matters.

We must help students understand that they *can* get better. But change consists of more than just the optimistic slogans we put on our walls and repeat every day, like "believe in yourself." What does that mean to our students who struggle? Positive messages only work if kids really understand how that can directly affect their progress. They need our help just like our staffs need our help, to make them understand they can accomplish anything if they have the right attitude and skills.

POSITIVE REINFORCEMENT AND THE PROBLEMS WITH PRIZES

Early on while teaching, I saw the effect that external rewards had on motivation in my students, especially when nothing else seemed to work. Frustrated in my inability to get my students to listen to me, I employed a reward system to inspire my students to want to be better behaved. Trying to be thrifty, I used laminated strips of colored construction paper as currency, like dollar bills, giving them out to students who met my class expectations. At the end of each week, students used their collection to "buy" various prizes as rewards. Consequently, the trinkets I initially used as rewards evolved, first into extra recess, then into activities as rewards, such as sitting in a special chair during class. Many of these changes were of necessity, because I couldn't afford to purchase prizes as a young teacher on a single income. I could barely afford my student loans and took my then girlfriend (now wife) on dates using the fast-food dollar menu (true story). First off, the idea that teachers have to fund their own prizes for behavioral systems is absurd. Any expense that is part of a classroom-management system should be funded by the school just like any reading or math program would be. This system I used was effective but had a limited long-term impact. I did really well with bribing students to behave, but I also observed how much my own mood each day played into how I rewarded, praised, and reinforced certain behaviors. When I handed out the paper strips like candy, I saw kids respond with more positive behaviors. If I failed to deliver, and didn't give as many out, I could visibly see the behavior deteriorate by the end of the day. In the end, I could see that the system worked, but really only worked as well as I used it.

I learned a lot from that experience of implementing a positive external reinforcement system in my classroom and have reflected on it so many times as I support teachers in their classrooms with their own style of management. These systems of using external rewards are a typical practice in Positive Behavior Interventions and Supports (PBIS), which is a research-based system that can be used to create a positive and rewarding environment for students. It's considered a must-have for reducing exclusionary discipline. One of the main aspects of PBIS is to use tangible incentives for students to motivate them to act in certain ways.

PBIS is based on the idea that students will choose to improve their own behaviors because they want the recognition and/or the reward that the staff use to entice them. Hopefully, over time, these behaviors transfer into habits that the students retain. PBIS takes us in the right direction toward highlighting and rewarding positive behavior instead of focusing on punishing misconduct.

Extrinsic motivation does get your students' attention and helps motivate them. Most importantly, it can help students form habits, even if they don't realize they are doing it. The *habits* are what we are really trying to target. Help students form productive and positive habits and their performance is guaranteed to increase. These systems are based on a behavioralist view of learning in which educators can use specific stimuli to control students' behaviors based on their desires or even change behaviors through repetition and association. We will explain these various theories in a later chapter. Positive-reward and -reinforcement systems are not the end-all goal but can be a great start when you don't know what else to do and you feel like you are drowning in your classroom.

But here's the thing: positive reinforcement works, but it only works as well as the reward's value to a student at any given moment. Physical toys and trinkets have to be constantly changed to keep the students interested in them. Many teachers use strategies like this, and they can be somewhat effective for many students. Fuzzies in a jar, fake money, stickers, and rewards for desired behavior can work. To reach all the students, there also must be many options, some very customized to specific students.

Then why shouldn't everyone use a reward system like this in every school and every classroom? Why isn't it mandated for all teachers? In some schools it is, but there are some problems with placing such a high emphasis on prizes for rewarding behavior. Unfortunately, our society is somewhat based on the idea that if we work hard, then we get things. It's built into capitalism and infects our classrooms. Kids walk in thinking, *What's in it for me*?

Alfie Kohn, in *Punished by Rewards: The Trouble with Gold Stars, Incentive Plans, A's, Praise, and Other Bribes*, describes how waving treats in front of students distracts them from their real goals. It teaches them to work toward rewards instead of for their own well-being. It motivates them, but motivates them to get the reward, not to consider their long-term goals. *Punished by Rewards* is a must-read when it comes to learning about the effect of external rewards.

Many of our current motivators have negative underlying consequences attached. Grades are a perfect example: If you do well, you get an A. But if you don't study (or you *do* study but still can't grasp the topic), you don't just not get an A, you get an F. These potential rewards are weighed down with negative reinforcements tied to the positive reinforcement. Students can see through this, and even when they get the positive reward, they still feel the potential threat of what would have happened if they didn't.

Using prizes focuses students on external rewards and distracts students from looking inward. Students will work toward prizes, but these do not provide the intrinsic connection and fulfillment that students really need and want. This is especially true for our most challenging students. Many times, they don't have the same concern intrinsically for others, for you, or even of their own well-being.

It reminds me of a scene in the 2006 movie *The Break-Up* with Jennifer Aniston and Vince Vaughn. Aniston's character is mad at Vaughn's character, her husband, because he doesn't want to help out around the house. "I don't want you to do the dishes, I want you to want to do the dishes," she says to him. He sees no value in doing the dishes and she is mad at him for it. His answer is priceless. "Why would I want to do dishes?" He doesn't learn until much later in the story how this attitude affects her. He is thinking in the here and now, and in his own self-interest. This is just like so many of our students. We want our students to not only do their work and behave, but also we want them to *want* to do their work and behave. We can't make them want to do something, but we can consider using motivators that are truly in the students' self-interest and are personally rewarding. When we reward students for very specific actions, we run the risk of forcing them to act in ways that only we think are appropriate.

Another major problem with using prizes is bias. The desired behaviors being rewarded are defined by the staff, who may have biases about what they deem "appropriate" and good. The creation of the system designed to "help the kids" rarely involves the kids in deciding the rules of the game, and the game ends up not being fair to many of our students, specifically the students that do not look like or talk like the staff. No matter what we do as educators, we have bias in defining the desired behaviors we are seeking. Extreme bias can turn into racism, which over time becomes institutionalized. It's essential to have your students and their parents help define any desired behavior. Also avoid vague terms such as "respect" and "responsible," since they tend to be very subjective.

When you use prizes or praise, consider a few tips:

Treat rewards **like giving a gift to a friend**: You can give, but never take it back once given. It's not effective to take away rewards the student has already earned. It sours the entire system and harms trust between staff and students.

Use **age-appropriate rewards.** Do your homework so you know what is appropriate based on research. Personalize your rewards based on the individual student, their interests, their age, and their goals.

Fade usage as students' skills develop. This is critical and often overlooked. The goal for any reinforcement plan should be *to use it only as necessary.* As soon as we can, we should wean off the rewards as the student demonstrates mastery of the new skills.

An Abundance of Verbal Praise

There is a difference between verbal praise and external trinkets, but they can be both used appropriately or inappropriately. Students need a ton of praise to reinforce desired behaviors. The more you use it, the more it will work.

If you are wondering if you are giving enough recognition for the behaviors you want, the answer is no. Do more. I never realized exactly how much and often just did what felt right to me. In fact, students need a four-to-one ratio of positive to negative feedback for their new behaviors to take hold and become habit. That means for every one negative comment or redirection of bad behavior, that same student needs four more comments of positive feedback. That can be really difficult at times, trying to find even one thing the child is doing right, but that's our job. The more you look for something, the more you will find it. If you can't see it, then you aren't looking hard enough. Every child is doing many positive behaviors that are often taken for granted.

Behavior-Specific Praise Statements

Additionally, make sure to use behavior-specific praise statements to maximize the impact of your praise. Don't just say, "Good job!" Instead, be very specific with what they did and how that connects to their success.

Say the student's name to get their attention. State what specific action the student did that you want to recognize. Make a connection to your class or school rules. Describe how it will help them be more successful in the long run. For examples, "Andy, you were really focused on taking notes during the lesson today. That shows that you were really attentive, one of our school characteristics. I can tell that you learned a lot and will be much more ready for the test this week."

It seems like it will take a lot longer, but as we become more comfortable with being more specific, we will do it faster and more efficiently.

SCHOOLWIDE HOUSE SYSTEMS

Many schools are using Harry Potter–style house systems, which have become popular all over the world and are based on this same principle of external rewards. Schools create groups of students. Staff reinforce the behaviors they have stated are appropriate and good using points. These points are tracked publicly and the winner over time is rewarded with prizes and celebrations. The idea is that the school is rewarded good behavior in hopes that all students will be influenced by watching their peers get the rewards and thus themselves also act "good" in the future.

Many of these house systems are extremely successful in turning around student behavior and increasing a more positive school culture. I would suggest a few tips if you are going to use this plan, both for improving it as a more effective strategy and to better understand the deeper impact it can have in your school.

First, discuss and decide as a team what the real goals are for this new system. Be specific and practical. What are you really trying to accomplish? List these goals out from the beginning and then periodically review if they are being met as you implement your system.

Second, again together with your staff, grow consensus on what the desired behaviors are going to be, and do this for each area of your school. These can and should be put into a chart that is typically called a behavior matrix. The list should only include behaviors that are fact-based and visible; subjective terms like "respect" should be avoided.

Third, create a plan for instruction with the staff. How will you teach those desired behaviors to the students before points are doled out and then reteach once you see that some students are not acting toward your desired behaviors? As you plan, consider how you can grow the skills *and the attitudes* that help kids be on task, focused, and actually nice to each other. There has to be teaching and learning behind any positive-reinforcement system you use for it to have a lasting effect on behavior.

Fourth, check yourself so that we are not using this to just control our students and wield power over them. As you model, teach, reteach, and support your students in learning new behaviors, help them also reflect on how their actions are aligned to personal, classroom, and school goals. We'll get into that more in the next section.

Fifth, these systems have to be more than just the points and celebrations. One of the reasons I actually love this strategy is for how it can pull a school together and grow the ideals of teamwork and family.

I actually personally feel that the aspect of giving out points has a minimal impact, but the relationships that can be formed between teachers and students are the real "win" in this scenario. When we connect staff and students from completely different grades and departments, it pulls together the feel of the school and helps even a large school feel like a tight community. For this effect to really grab hold, it's all about *how* you implement it more than *what* you actually do. If you are going to celebrate, *then really celebrate.* Be all in. Give yourself to your peers and students *with your whole heart.* Be in the moment when recognizing others. If you do this program halfway, you won't even get half-results. It will basically give you zero results, if not make things worse. Your school has to fully commit to doing this with passion for it to really work. It's all or nothing.

No matter what you use, focus more on the instruction of the desired behaviors than the rewards. We need to work with students and help them see how their actions affect their goals instead of trying to manipulate them into doing what we want.

REGULATING EXTERNAL INFLUENCE

Emotions affect actions. I grew up in the 1980s during the self-esteem craze. In class, we participated in what I considered silly activities that focused on how special everyone was. It was similar to the common "everyone gets a trophy" mentality that bothers so many people today, but there was a reason why this movement started in the first place. This is often misunderstood and even mocked in popular culture. Stuart Smalley on *Saturday Night Live* had his catchphrase: "I'm good enough. I'm smart enough. And doggone it, people like me!"

While it may be funny, and even now we make fun of it, there is truth in Smalley's line. We can't dismiss the importance of our students' sense of self. If we dismiss this internal struggle, we are dismissing the child's humanity.

As educators, we must be extremely mindful of the words we say to students and intentional with repeating phrases and stories that we want them to remember. We must help students and staff that struggle understand how their own emotions affect them and that they need to regulate those emotions if they want to move forward with their skills. Emotions and actions have a vicious and powerful impact on each other every single day. If our emotions are going in the wrong direction, it's sometimes not enough just to *want* to change them. Sometimes we need to instead focus on our actions, our daily routines, and our habits in order to feel different about ourselves.

Sometimes focusing entirely on our emotions is the key, and we need to be intentional in our self-talk and the influences coming at us and around us. It could be that the people we talk to most often, and who influence us the most, are who we need to change. It could be what we watch or listen to that needs to change. These environmental factors affect our emotions, which in turn affect our actions.

When you are working with your students, take some time to help them reflect on these inputs coming into their daily lives. What shows are they watching? What are they seeing on the internet? What games are they playing? These are not always direct causes of misconduct, but research has shown they do have an effect on how people view the world around them.

As we discussed earlier in the book, we can use social learning to be a positive influence on our students and their behaviors. Unfortunately, the world has been trying to influence them since they were born and many of those influences are not healthy. Let's talk about some aspects of how we may be controlled without even realizing it.

We Believe What We Repeatedly Watch

One example is the *Cultivation Theory*, by sociologist George Gerbner in the 1960s, which explains how people are influenced by the media that they view for long periods of time. In practice, the more media that we consume, the more our perceptions change based on that media. We start believing the reality of what we see, regardless of how true it is. Consider the impact of someone having their favorite news channel constantly playing in the background throughout the day and how that affects their political world view.

We have to help students understand how certain media they may obsess over, like adult anime or inappropriate video games, can warp their perspectives. It's not that we need to completely stop their interest or viewership, but even if we can get them to be more conscious about how much they view it, it can be a win.

We Become What We See Others Do

One of the most powerful influencers, especially for teenagers, is peer pressure, also called peer persuasion. In the 1950s, Polish American psychologist Solomon Asch conducted multiple studies to observe how adults reacted to purposeful misdirection by peers or authority figures. These were called the *conformity experiments*. In one experiment, he placed a small group of adults in a room and had them verbally answer easy questions on a vision test aloud in front of others. Only one individual was truly being experimented on and what he didn't know was that Asch had already hired the rest of the group to intentionally answer most of the questions incorrectly. The subject of the experiment watched his peers and had to decide whether or not to go against the group in answering the questions aloud. Asch found that, most of the time, those experimented on purposefully answered questions incorrectly even though they knew they were wrong. When asked later, they explained why they did this. As adults they knew the answer was wrong, but they just wanted to fit in with the group or even doubted their own answers, thinking that maybe the rest of the group knew something they didn't.

Students make decisions for a variety of reasons and may do things they know are wrong but feel enormous peer pressure to do. Peer pressure isn't always just overt and direct coercion. It often is subtle group-think. I call this *the mob mentality*.

I'm not referencing the Mafia. More like a massive herd of animals, unpredictable and fickle as a group. As classroom and school leaders, we need to control the mob, to consider the individual and group simultaneously. If we can sway a group positively, then a huge majority of the group continues to act nicer to others, even individual students who may at times misbehave. If the group tends to go negative, then kids that may otherwise act appropriate will instead act in ways out of their character. This is why we can't have effective disciplinary programs unless we have a positive and safe school culture. Additionally, students act in ways that their friends act, so it helps to pull their friends into the mix when helping redirect behavior.

REGULATORS, MOUNT UP!

Our students will instinctively respond with fight, flight, or freeze when confronted with something they consider threatening. This is a natural and physiological reaction. As we have already discussed, external negative factors *do* influence kids and *will* often trigger this type of non-thinking response in them. Many times, the reason that we are working with them is exactly because these automatic reactions were ones that caused misconduct, disruptions, and arguments with peers. It would be so easy if when we met with them, they just totally admitted their wrongdoing, owned their fault, and explained ways they would right their wrongs. Not likely, right? Instead, we hear them blaming the victim. Or they displace the responsibility of their actions due to environmental factors or others' behaviors. They may even justify their actions by trying to explain how they were really in the right. Worse, they may not even care about any consequences from their behavior that come their way.

Ultimately, though, our end game is to develop their *agency*, or their cognitive choice on which actions to take next to reach their goals regardless of the negative external challenges. Empowering this internal sense of control takes forethought, intentionality, self-reflection, and self-regulation. It takes time.

Students with a strong sense of agency are constantly regulating their own emotions and decisions even through difficult times. Our way to teach this level of self-regulation is through coregulation, or our modeling, practicing, and coaching of new strategies *together* with the student in order to influence their later responses to internal anxiety or anger. It always starts with us. *We* need to be effective self-regulators, so it's time to mount up.

Using Gradual Release to Teach Coregulation

So what does coregulation look like in a class or with a teacher? I think the simplest and most common-sense approach is to use a process we already know from other academic subjects, the gradual release model. Gradual release as a philosophy is easy to understand, but we often speed through from "I do," barely touching on "we do," and then focus too much on "you do." To help you remember the importance of each phase of the process, I have a new way of thinking about it: Me, We, See.

Me: Every skill we want our kids to learn must first start with how we talk, act, and behave toward them. Great improvements in others must start with "me." It's a reminder that we can't really force change in others, but our work is more about inspiring them to want to improve themselves. Model for them how to regulate emotions with your breathing, calming strategies, and use of calming tools. One time is not enough. Not even close. If students learn effectively the more they watch something, then we need to think more like YouTube and celebrate how many views we get. Model, model, model.

Another way to model self-regulation is by sharing stories of times you were stressed, had high anxiety, or were really upset. You don't have to get too personal with details but share what you did to help yourself feel better. Was it reading a book, taking a walk, or deep breathing? Help students by relating to their concerns and showing them what worked for you based on your own tough times. It also allows them to see that they are not alone in their struggles and that, just like you, they can get through them, too.

We: Guided practice should be intentional and personalized. Work together to brainstorm areas of their lives that often frustrate them or increase anxiety. Help them think of things they can do to relax in different settings they might find themselves in. In school, relaxing can be hard because students are limited in what they are allowed to do in class. Maybe a child needs a special pass to see the counselor or another mentor teacher. Maybe they need a calm corner where they can get away from others in class for minute. Maybe they are allowed to do other work at their desk even though it's technically off task. When we help them think of these strategies, we can also help make the solutions on our terms and something we can live with.

See: Create typical scenarios that you can use as prompts to see how they respond. Coach them through their reactions as if they were really in the situation. Do this in the areas where the issues would occur to make it as realistic as possible. Your friend talked bad about you behind your back. What are you going to do? Someone tried to trip you as you walked through the hallway. What are you going to do? Your parents screamed at you all morning before school started. You just arrived at school. What are you going to do? Their thinking and reflection matter just as much as any specific tool we may use, especially the older the student. It's the brain we are trying to develop, the cognitive choice. By allowing students to talk these through in a safe and low-stress environment, we can help make them routine, so that when they are tested in real life, they will be more likely to make better decisions independently.

Intentional Breathing

Mindfulness through breathing and meditation are popular in our society as ways for adults to intentionally de-stress. The app Calm, now worth over a billion dollars, is one of the most successful examples of how much more accepted this is.

Regulating breathing is one of the most important skills adults can have. And it's one of the first things we should teach our students. We often ask kids to breathe when they get upset, but they don't even know what that means. They *are* breathing. All the time. We don't simply want them to breathe, but to slow down and *concentrate* on their breathing.

BREATHING BREAKS

ROLLER COASTER
Trace your fingers with your opposite hand. Trace up your fingers and breathe in, trace down your fingers and breathe out. Also called Five Finger Breathing.

CANDLES
Hold up all your fingers. Blow them out like birthday cake candles one by one.

TUMBLE DRYER
Point index fingers overlapping towards each other in front of your face. Rotate your fingers around each other quickly, blow softly, and listen to the swishing.

HOT SOUP
Smell the soup and breathe in. Softly blow off the steam and breathe out. Vary using cocoa or flowers: smell the flowers and breathe in and blow off the petals by breathing out.

WHOLE BODY
Breathe in while raising your arms at your side all the way above your head. Breathe out while slowly lowering your arms to your side.

TRIANGLE
Breath in 3 seconds, hold 3 seconds, breathe out 3 seconds. Repeat. Vary by having students trace the triangle or trace an imaginary triangle in the air.

BOX
Breathe in 4 seconds, hold 4 seconds, breathe out 4 seconds, hold 4 seconds. Repeat. Vary by having students trace the box or trace an imaginary box in the air.

LAZY EIGHT
Slowly breathe in while tracing the left side of the lazy eight. Then slowly breathe out tracing the right side of the lazy eight.

This needs to be taught and practiced when times are easy. Don't introduce methods like these only when kids are upset. By then, it's usually too late to avoid disruptive behaviors. Instead, teach actions and routines associated with mindful breathing to help create a pattern for how students take breaths. Many apps have a timer and visuals that can be adjusted to suit your needs and interests. These apps are great for older students and adults. Students and adults at all ages can benefit from breathing strategies. In the upper grade levels, work with the whole class to discuss and create strategies that are more subtle, or gather students into small groups to create more focused mindful breathing practices. There are creative ways to keep the interest of younger students and help them focus only on breathing and not the many issues they are dealing with at the time.

Break Stations

Students are stuck. Stuck in a school or classroom all day. Forced to be there, feeling like they have no power, no control, and like they are so constrained that they physically and emotionally burst sometimes. The pressure that builds up needs to be released slowly and on their terms.

One way to do this is to create a station in your classroom or your school where students can take optional, scheduled breaks. These go by different names in different schools: reset rooms, connect corners, calm corners, etc. These areas typically are calm areas, have sensory materials, or distracting items to help students refocus or de-stress. This could be anything from a Starbucks-style lounge in high school to a LEGO wall in an elementary school.

Sensory rooms have become an increasingly popular example of this. Sensory rooms have specialized lighting, sounds, and materials that stimulate sensory needs. Our sensory room has two large bubble machines that light up different colors, a sound machine that plays white noise, and a variety of different seating options like bean bags, rocking chairs, and even gaming seats on the floor. There are also sequin sheets and other materials (carpet, turf, Velcro, and corduroy)

SHIFT FROM EXTERNAL REWARDS TO SELF-REGULATION

on the wall for students to run their hands over. Students helped us choose our equipment. We purchased some items and brought them in and then listened to and watched student reactions. As we learned what they preferred, our room developed accordingly. Sometimes, it's helpful to have even more specialized equipment like body socks and weighted blankets, depending on the special needs of your students.

If you are designing a new building, before you automatically put in typical spaces like a computer lab, perhaps consider replacing one with a sensory room. It can be viewed as another way to help potentially disruptive students learn how to help themselves.

In our school, we have a variety of activities throughout the building. I love the idea of schools feeling like a children's museum, with hands-on activities throughout the building. For example, we used a blower and dryer ducting to create our air station. Students place colored scarves inside the tubes and watch them travel though one hundred feet of tubing to then pop out toward the ceiling and slowly travel to the ground. It's very visual and engaging, and it often turns students' mood around quickly. We have sensory paths with stickers on the floor so students can jump and tiptoe through a winding maze. We have LEGO walls with LEGO boards attached to them so students can build off the wall. Consider creating things in your building that can be intentional in the distraction they create. This might seem counterintuitive because we don't want to distract from learning, but giving students creative, interesting breaks helps them take their minds off their problems and reduces their stress, thus reducing their disruptive behavior.

Sensory Bins

We should also be prepared to give our students breaks so that they don't always have to leave the classroom to calm down or self-regulate.

Sensory bins, or "chill chests," are a great solution. These bins contain a variety of tools for self-regulation that students can use while listening to instruction and remaining in the classroom. Many kids can do two things at once and need to. For example, I've seen kids who can't sit still, so teachers allow them to read while they are listening to instruction.

An outsider might look at this and judge it, thinking the kid isn't getting any new learning. But when you follow up, you realize the students really did understand what was going on. This is not always the right strategy (it depends on the student, the age, and the situation), but don't dismiss the need for some kids to multitask.

To create a sensory bin, start by finding an area in your classroom where you can put it. The bin can be a box, basket, or plastic bin with lid. We used 10" × 6" clear bins with lids so that you can see the contents from the outside. Use a timer to provide limits for students in this area. Include a variety of sensory materials in the bin. Items that worked for us were anything with fuzzy material or something with sequins that they could rub one way for one color and then rub the other way for a different color. From there, keep adding things that kids like to use and rotate items in and out: stress balls, pinwheels, and a Hoberman sphere (our kids' favorite). Put a list of breathing strategies and self-regulation tips in the bin, but make sure you practice these if you want the kids to use them on their own. Finally, add a few books focused on social stories for self-regulation and for dealing with emotions to each bin. We bought each grade level a set and rotated a few books for each class around throughout the year. Students can bring their own sensory or calming items or habits to the area. For some kids, it may be sitting and reading. For others, it may be fidgeting. Each child is different, so different options are essential.

Intentional Movement

Many of our kids can't sit still—so don't make them! Get them moving and work their bodies.

My escape growing up was playing basketball. I would take my ball and ride my bike one handed, holding my basketball in the other hand, to the courts as often as I could. Snow, rain, sun, it didn't matter.

Getting out and moving helped me forget about any problems I had and let me block out the noise. Did it solve any problems I had? No. But it did get my mind off them for a while and helped me get to a base level of calm.

Sometimes you need to intentionally stop thinking about something in order to come up with a solution. Games and physical activities are engaging to the body, which focuses the mind, releases endorphins, and creates a sense of calm.

Can you create a bank of physical activities? Pick both highly physical and less physical activities. They can be used as a scheduled intervention, like having students be active every day at a scheduled time. This can also be done as an in-the-moment distraction. Instead of just taking students out of class and sitting them in your office to talk about why they yelled at their classmate and threw their book across the room, take them to the basketball court and let them shoot hoops with you as they discuss what happened. You will have a very different conversation.

Anytime you bring students' energy levels up, just make sure to also find ways to bring them back down before returning to classwork. Deep breathing, read alouds, drawing, and repetitive mindfulness activities can help do this.

REDIRECTION VS. REWARD DILEMMA

"But why are we giving in to students so much? Why do kids get rewarded for bad behavior?" These are the most common responses to strategies where we provide fun and engaging experiences for students who misbehave.

Nothing drives teachers crazier than feeling like a student who has been highly disruptive and disrespectful was rewarded for these behaviors. The key thing to remember is that we must first deal with emotions—our students' and our own—before dealing with the behaviors. As psychologist and author Dr. Bruce Perry suggests, we must first regulate, then relate, and then finally reason. The longer we fight the battle, the longer it will take to get to some common understanding. Students are not ready to listen and learn if they are at a heightened stress level. No one can focus when their mind is in chaos.

Getting their attention is critical. Is offering a preferred activity rewarding negative behavior? It can be—and that's why we don't often do it. But when we are stuck, we need to be creative and take baby steps to move forward together. So, ahead of time, know what students' preferred activities are. Have a list and have the materials. Use time limits so the student knows that this is a short-term break before getting back into the issue. The important point is that we must first get students to a base level of calm before dealing with a problem. Students can't learn if they are not calm.

Society is often out to get our kids. They need agency to fend for themselves and learn to create a better life. They need help regulating their emotions, not controlling them. Like a pressure-release valve, they can adjust the flow of the emotions if they know how. Emotions are part of what makes our kids special and unique as human beings. Have go-to strategies that we know are effective readily available. As we model and practice these techniques, our students will begin to develop the self-regulation strategies they can take with them for the rest of their lives.

TIME-OUT

> To help others, we must consider what helps ourselves. What do you watch? Who do you talk to the most? How does this influence your thoughts and feelings about life? Should you adjust something in your life to better control how you feel?

> What are some ways that you can help your students be more aware of the influences in their lives?

> What is one thing you can do to help your students grow agency by learning how to regulate emotions?

CHAPTER 8

ALLOW STUDENTS TO BE LEADERS OF CHANGE

DISCIPLINE ISN'T SOMETHING YOU DO TO CHILDREN, IT'S SOMETHING YOU DEVELOP WITHIN THEM. –DR. BECKY BAILEY

We once had a student who was giving us a hard time every morning on his way to class. Each day, he would somehow find every wrong turn and distracting behavior he could, often pulling others along with him. It quickly became clear that we needed to come up with a plan to redirect this behavior.

We started with reteaching and reviewing the expectations. When that didn't change the behavior, we knew we had to step up our game before we ended up with a consequence-driven reaction on our part. So we looked at the situation and some root causes of the behavior. What we found was that the student had a tremendous amount of free time walking to his homeroom class. Did he really need to do that independently? Well, we didn't want to make a staff member escort him, since he would just push back and feel untrusted. What else could we do?

Sometimes the answer is to stop, reframe your thinking of the child, and instead treat them as if they are a very well-behaved child. What would you do with them then? The answer, in this case, was leadership.

So, I gave this student a job. He was our new crossing guard helping families walk safely to school. He was trained by one of our teachers, and we made him part of our car rider line team.

Watching him work was captivating. He was so good. Positive, helpful, kind. He welcomed kids into school, helped parents cross the crosswalk, and guided younger students to class. The added responsibility put his energy to work. It also showed him that we trusted him and viewed him as good and capable. We saw the kid we knew was hidden beneath the previous misbehavior, just desperate to have a reason to come out. The busy-ness of his "job" naturally kept him from getting in trouble, and by the time he was done, he had to hurry to class in empty hallways free from distraction.

SHARING POWER, NOT GIVING IT AWAY

It goes without saying, but it's worth repeating: No one wins in a power struggle. The real step in "winning" is to realize that you win when the child wins, or in other words, when the child is making progress, meeting their goals, and achieving new positive outcomes. We can still retain authority while allowing students to empower themselves if we lead instead of mandate change. In fact, we can gain more respect by sharing power, control, and ownership with our students. It's an essential component of self-improvement and a fundamental theme of this book. Helping students own their development will allow them to see how their actions impact progress toward their goals. Just like we would want to be treated, we need to give our students grace and space to work through this on a regular basis.

Richard Lavoie, in his book *The Motivation Breakthrough*, discusses how educators can rethink power in the classroom. He argues that there are many defiant students who yearn for more power and control of their own lives in school. This then causes power struggles with educators, who fight for control of their classroom or school. Students that push for power often have many aspects of their personal lives in chaos or at least they feel stuck in someone else's choices, not their own. Students don't typically choose their class, their peers, their school environment, or their teachers. Students that fight for power feel this lack of control intensely and will try to gain control through any means possible, often in ways that are disruptive to us. As Lavoie states, the need that some students have for more control of their lives can be intense and cause them to be noncompliant, stubborn, or resistant to rules.

Something that helps me with these students is to remind myself that this need for control and power is just that, a need. It's not a want. It's like any other basic need: food, water, love, choice, and safety. When we reframe this push for control as a need, it helps us to reconsider what we do in response.

As educators, we also have this need for control and power in our classrooms. And I'm not saying there is anything wrong with that, but it's important to remember the difference between *power* and *authority*. Great teachers own their environment and everything in it. They understand that they can retain authority without making the students feel like they are being controlled or micromanaged. Great teachers are on it. They know exactly what they want and how to get it. But I think one of the main reasons that educators are concerned or even scared of letting go is that they are so determined to do a great job in the classroom, and so they hold on to the thing they love too tightly. As we reflect on our own need for power and control, let's understand that when students and teachers both need control, there will be some natural conflict that occurs. The main way to address this is to be pro-active and give students what they need—in this case more power and control in their own lives—*but in a way that works for us, too.*

I think there is a problem in thinking of this as power that we can give or take. A better way to think of it is as leadership, where we are doing our best to motivate and inspire students to *want* to make improvements in their lives, in their classrooms, and in their schools. The battle for power and control in the classroom is a trap for educators. Teachers, administrators, and parents can't really control the students anyways. Only the students themselves control what they do. We are not giving them control or power. They already have it. They are born with it, entitled to it, and need us to show them how to handle it and use it properly. The more we try to hang on to all of the power, the more students fight to have their own. Ultimately, like Richard Lavoie stated so well, "Kids don't want your power, they want their own." Students that feel like they are allowed to use the power they feel within themselves to affect the world around them will be less likely to fight you for it.

STUDENT OWNERSHIP

We should expect and want our students to flex their personal sense of control with us, but we had better help them learn to do it in the right way or that flexing will turn disruptive. First, develop their perceived and actual control of their environment. This means giving them more choice and voice in the classroom and school. It means allowing them the freedom to change the environment or instruction to better suit their needs.

Give Power to Students through Leadership

As students age and develop, they naturally challenge authority to gain more power for themselves. Some students do this much more than others. Some of the kids that push us the most will be our best leaders when they get older, especially if we help them learn positive leadership skills along the way. Let's talk about how we can intentionally and strategically empower our students in ways that create meaningful positive changes in their lives.

Provide Minor Choices

Adding choices does not mean creating separate lesson plans for every child or giving many different ways to do the same project. While those things can be helpful, they're unrealistic for daily lessons. Consider choices as a means to an end. Some of our students just don't want to do what they are told, almost out of spite. If we give them a couple of choices about how they complete an activity or participate, they might see the situation much differently. Now, all of a sudden, they have some power and can control their next steps.

Sometimes the choices can be the method of work completion, for instance writing vs. drawing. Other times, it can be a choice to participate in a group project or to work independently. The key thing is for the teacher to not feel that one way or another is better. Let it go. Let them pick. Then help them maximize their choice. One way to live with students' choices as a teacher is to give them clear parameters, such as time for completion or success criteria. This way, it still comes back to everyone achieving similar learning outcomes. The outcomes should drive the choices.

Give Input to the Rules and Procedures

Many disciplinary situations can be prevented if schools use effective processes to gain feedback, input, and consensus from students to create the rules in the first place. Dress code is a great example. It's a perfect storm of preferences, cultural norms, and conservative viewpoints that must be figured out to come up with a general agreement on what is proper attire. Schools sometimes make these decisions in isolation or follow traditional rules and then don't know how to address violations when they occur. When did it become the school's job to regulate clothing in this way? Is this really the best use of our time?

Problems that pop up every day, like dress-code violations or cell phone usage, can seem small but end up taking a lot of time from the school to discipline and leave the students feeling misunderstood and isolated. I believe the best way to monitor your own implicit bias about how we interpret and enact the rules in school is to involve the students and other stakeholders as much as possible in creating those norms and then monitoring the implementation of them. Consider these tips for making new rules or reflecting on the ones you have:

> **Define**: Write the rule in positive language, focusing on what you want kids to do, not what you want them not to do. Be as specific and clear as you can with what it looks like and sounds like.

> **Explain**: Write down the purpose of this rule. There must be a reason this rule is being added, right? Right? Sometimes we have rules just because we have always had them. If you don't have a clear purpose for a rule, get rid of it! How does this rule benefit students and the school? Reflect on whether you really need this rule after all. What if we didn't have this rule? Would the environment be much different?

> **Predict**: When a rule is implemented, what will likely happen with most students? Can you think of any that will likely struggle based on this expectation? List any groups of students or specific students that might struggle when this rule is implemented. Why would they struggle? Is it due to a disability or cultural difference? Are they of different ethnicity or race from you? Then go back and redefine the rule or plan for ways to support and teach the students toward success.

Reflect: Take a minute and review every rule you have for any cultural or racial bias. There are many aspects of cultures that you may not be thinking of when you are making rules. We should always be listening to our families to learn more about their cultural norms as well as staying abreast of new learning on this topic. But it could be as simple as googling the rule and seeing what comes up. What has happened in other schools implementing this same rule? Don't be surprised by something you weren't thinking about.

Students are often ignored in the planning phase of discipline, or not trusted enough to give valuable insight into their experiences. When students take ownership for changes, they embrace these changes even when you are not around. Give your students say in creating the school plan.

Don't overlook small things that students can lead. The more they own the process or environment, the more they will protect it like their own. One time, a young man was concerned that we didn't have dividers between the urinals in the boys' bathroom and it was causing a commotion in the bathroom. He wanted more privacy for all the kids involved and to end the fights that were going on between kids. This was something that made a lot of sense to me, so I asked him to work with one of our student leaders to create a proposal for this change. He researched what was needed, including the cost, and made a presentation. He shared this with the school's advisory council, they agreed, and we purchased and installed the new dividers. The young man was there from start to finish. He was part of this change and owned it. He gained confidence and began participating more in class after this experience.

Allow Students to Learn and Grow from Mistakes

Students that push for power typically also push our buttons and our boundaries. This is not always intentional. They overstep. They assume they are in charge and can be bossy. They test their limits. Having enormous patience as an educator is so important, because if we can help students understand how their words and actions affect others, we can teach them through these mistakes how to be better people in the future.

When I was in high school, I was nominated for the National Honor Society due to my grades and involvement in the school. If you looked at my academic résumé, I should have been a shoo-in for acceptance. But I was a behavioral problem for my teachers at times. OK, many times. I was not always the best behaved, so they denied me access to this "elite" club. I wasn't given a reason why, although I could take a good guess. No staff member ever explained it to me or tried to help me understand. Did I "deserve" it? I don't know, maybe. But did it "teach me a lesson"? Definitely not. Whatever lesson they were trying to teach me only made me feel more disconnected. *Why help a school that won't include you?* That's what I thought at the time. I believe so strongly that when we get too tough and limit the opportunities for our students due to their past mistakes, we can accidentally create the thing we don't want the most.

We should be careful that we don't use student leadership "contracts" to become just another tool to hold kids accountable that can be used against them when they make a mistake. I'm admittedly a bleeding heart when it comes to my kids, but I'd rather err on the side of second chances than lose the students altogether. When students overstep their boundaries, educators should maximize learning instead of threats.

Help Students Align their Habits to Long-Term Goals

A key step for change is helping students identify their personal goals and criteria for success. Success to educators may look different than it does to students. Help them think long term and big picture first and then lead them into what is needed now for them to get to their dreams later in life. Below are some examples of questions you can ask to help your students think toward their long-term goals.

> What is your dream for your life when you are an adult? What do you want to do for a living to make money and support your family? What activities and hobbies do you think you would like to do then?
>
> Looking at your dreams, what skills do you think are important for those jobs and activities? Do you have those skills already? What things can we do now to help prepare you? What things can we maybe take off your plate in school to help you focus on these skills instead?
>
> Let's list three things we can do right now to help remind you how to improve yourself, so you are working toward your goal instead of away from it. Let's list exactly *what* you would like to do and *when* you are doing to do it.

The key is to find common goals both for the school and student. Help them understand how your goals for them should truly be their goals as well. It works both ways. Their goals for themselves should also be our goals for them as well. The plan you create together will be more effective if you have clear steps that align to those hopes and dreams. When students believe that extra work is in their own best interest, they will invest in your shared plan.

You really need to set time aside to work this out with them. When done right, students should have their own folders or notebooks that list out their goals, why they are important to the student, small new routines that will help them achieve their goals, and celebrations planned for when they meet them. I know when I've rushed through this process in the past it became less meaningful. Don't let it be another box to check off on the to-do list. Kids can tell when that's happening. It's also important to do this kind of work when things are calm and not in the middle of a crisis.

Let Students Own their Progress: Student-Led Conferences

Student-led conferences can completely change the culture of your school and the outcomes for your students. I've seen this work so well in our school and others, that I don't know at this point how it can't be the new norm everywhere.

In traditional parent-teacher conferences, staff and parents meet to review the academic and sometimes behavioral progress of the child. Students are not involved directly and thus cannot give their input or even hear the conversation being had about them. Student-involved or student-led conferences bring the student into the conversation, literally giving them a seat at the table, so that we are talking with them, not about them. Why is this important? When students are actively involved in organizing, presenting, and sharing their own progress in school, they are guaranteed to be more invested in their progress and feel that their input really is valued.

There are two different methods for student-focused conferences: student-involved and student-led conferences.

Student-involved conferences are similar to traditional conferences, but instead of excluding students from the room, students have an equal voice, share their thoughts and feelings, and hear direct feedback from their parents and teachers. Since the students are involved, they can give insight into *why* they may not be successful and *what* they really need in the future.

For a student-led conference, students prepare the agenda, what they will share, and how they will share it. Even our youngest students and students with significant disabilities can lead their own conferences. I've seen it, and students do rise to the occasion. It's important to give the students structure so they are set up for success. I've listed a few items below to get you started.

1. Plan ahead and organize each step well in advance of the conference.

2. Prepare through practice. Give students time to practice with peers or with you ahead of time. Give them feedback. Scaffold this for different levels of students by using sentence starters or scripts.

3. Promote reviewing the progress of the child as a whole. This is not just about what they are struggling in. Make sure to discuss strengths and successes as well, no matter how much the child is having a difficult time in school.

4. Parents may have their own experiences, both good and bad, with parent-teacher conferences in the past. Advocate for this new method by selling it to the parents ahead of time so they know what to expect.

5. Allow follow-up meetings with families that need to be separate from the child. There are unique and sensitive circumstances that require private conversations. Just be careful to not use this as a reason to *not* do the student-involved conference altogether. Do both.

6. Push through any parent negativity by just doing an amazing job preparing and setting kids up for success.

One time, we had a parent who refused to bring his child to the conference, forcing us to do it, in his words, "old school." Sitting there waiting for his conference, he saw other students and parents highly engaged in the process, positive, and leaving highly satisfied. Before we knew it, he left and quickly returned with his child in tow.

I hope that if nothing else, you incorporate student-led conferences into your list of strategies in your school. Conferences like these are great throughout the year, not just as an annual event. They are extremely effective at any age level, not just for the student, but also as a reminder to us that students should be in front of everything we do.

Allow Students to Help Others as Peer Coaches

Students should never be used to replace the instruction from a highly qualified teacher, but peer coaching is a great strategy to provide students with support and reteaching from peers. Behaviorally, peers can model and explain how to act and what to do in specific situations. Peers can also be a go-to support for students when the teacher is unavailable.

Peer coaches need to be taught how to help and what to do in advance. They also need to be stronger in an area than the student in need. Consider choosing students that can relate to what students in need are going through. Older students who are now behaving appropriately but previously had similar behavioral issues are great resources.

Make sure to be diverse in how you choose your models, coaches, and leaders for other students. Perception is reality. If students feel that you choose out of bias, then you are. In other words, are students in these leadership positions all the same gender, race, or ability? It helps to have a process of monitoring each year who we are considering as the "good kids" and why they are chosen. Bias creeps up on us when we are not paying attention.

Too many times we use the "good kids" as peer mentors, but in many cases these kids are not the best ones to use. They may not even be able to understand or talk to the issues that the younger students are going through. Help the conversations by providing structure. Tools like sentence starters are great ways to provide structure to peer coaching and can be used by students when they need help or by coaches when they are giving help.

Create a New System of School Discipline through a Youth Court

My friend Dr. Kevin Armstrong is the executive principal at DuPont Hadley Middle School and a Fellow for the NAESP Center of Middle

Level Leadership. He has a unique way of incorporating student leadership as a discipline process called youth court. Youth court is an innovative way of sharing authority by granting a team of students decision-making powers in a process regarding their peers' discipline. Here's how Dr. Armstrong describes it:

> While youth courts can take various forms, in the restorative justice model this will provide a youth-led process to help young people understand the harm their actions have caused to others and to their community, take steps to repair that harm, and learn to make better decisions in the future. In contrast to suspension, detention, or other punishments, youth courts reinforce membership in the community.
>
> The goals of Hadley Court are simple, but the impact stretched farther than we ever could have imagined. These goals are:
>
> - Students helping students make better decisions.
> - Transforming school environment.
> - Student empowerment.
>
> These goals have driven this program for the last four years. We have seen a dramatic drop in office referrals, bullying incidents, school suspensions, and expulsions.

Youth Court is a great example of using students as leaders to make meaningful change in school. In Kevin's school, the more minor disciplinary situations are held by administrators to be presented instead at their Youth Court after school. Students are provided time to explain their "case" and then the students of the court make a decision based on the school code of conduct. When students own the conduct in their school, amazing things happen not only with student leaders, but with the entire student body.

WHO ARE YOUR STUDENT LEADERS?

It's healthy to annually review who your school considers as student leaders. Equal opportunity is one of those things we can control and monitor. Consider the questions below to guide you.

1. Are the student leaders representative of your student body in regard to race, culture, gender, and ability?
2. How are students selected for leadership roles in the first place? Are there any barriers to these opportunities? If you notice that a specific subgroup of kids don't apply, what can you do to reach out and include them?
3. What happens when students are in leadership roles and they misbehave?

Consider your own life's journey and how much you have felt in or out of control. How has that affected your investment and buy-in for things happening around you? Consider how effective it can be to move students from passive recipients of their learning and growing into active leaders, not just of their own lives, but of those around them as well.

This isn't a "strategy" like others we have discussed. Promoting student leadership is a philosophy of trust, that means looking beyond past transgressions and never giving up hope that all of our students can lead.

Thank you for giving your kids second chances! And for giving them third and fourth and fifth chances, too! Thank you for never giving up on a kid, no matter what they have done in the past. Every child has the ability to lead and help your school. In fact, some of our most challenging students can be the best leaders, but they need our help to use these skills for good.

Give kids a chance (again and again) and they will prove you right every time.

TIME-OUT

> What opportunities do your behaviorally challenged students have to lead their conferences, their learning, and their peers? If you don't have many opportunities now, which ones will you focus on in the future?

> How could you incorporate a youth court, involving students either in creation of the rules and/or decisions on how they are enforced?

CHAPTER 9

CREATE POWERFUL PARTNERSHIPS WITH PARENTS

GOOD LEADERS MUST FIRST BECOME GOOD SERVANTS.—ROBERT GREENLEAF

I once did a home visit to try and make a connection with a struggling student's dad after having difficulty connecting via phone or email. As I drove into his neighborhood, I realized he lived in a trailer park. Pulling through the gravel roads in my truck, I navigated to his home and immediately saw the student through the window. He was eating cereal, wearing sweats and bunny slippers, and watching TV. I knocked on the door and learned that his dad—his only parent—wasn't home yet. Instead of going in and putting us both in an uncomfortable situation, I waited patiently leaning against my tailgate.

The dad pulled up in his truck soon after, and quickly eyed me up. His own history with authority was obvious right away. I greeted him and explained that I was there to catch up on a couple of issues at school. I've learned to make sure parents know right away why I am connecting and that I am there to help. Reassuring parents is 90 percent of our job as educators and school leaders. We had a great talk at his kitchen table and worked out a few ideas that they could use at home. Mostly we formed a positive relationship and real connection. He even offered me a beer to celebrate our relationship, something I begrudgingly declined.

In that single visit, I learned a couple huge things. First, every day this child comes to school knowing that he lives in a trailer whereas other kids live in more expensive homes. He knows he has disadvantages. His "normal" at home was very different from the "normal" of many of our other students. Second, every day this child fends for himself while his dad is at work. There is no one helping him with homework or following up on school issues. He didn't have a fancy desk setup or calendar of assignments on the wall. Survival, not school, was the focus of their lives.

Home visits can be powerful tools. Knowing your students and their situations gives you perspective on how to best connect to them. Every time I suggest a home visit to teachers, I get sideways looks and a question: "We can do that?" I get it. It can be daunting, and it's a little scary to get out of our comfort zones, but just remember that meaningful relationships are built by extending trust. Willingness to go visit a family shows them how much you care.

When we learn about kids and what they are going through, it gives us context. If you want to reach out to a child, reach out to their entire family. Get to know them on their terms, not just yours. What you see in school is just one part of their life. Seeing them in their home environment gives you a whole new perspective on their situation.

DRIVEWAY DISCIPLINE

Like so many other schools, COVID-19 crushed our typical connections in school, so instead we went above and beyond to visit families at their homes. It was exhausting but really motivating for both staff and families. We used a tool that offered connection even without going inside people's homes, and in just a few minutes, we learned so much about what life looked like for our students. In many cases, we met grandparents and other relatives that lived in the home as well.

My friend middle school principal Beth Houf, coauthor of *Lead Like a PIRATE*, first used the term "driveway discipline" to refer to the work she and other leaders were doing to build relationships with families by implementing quick home visits and meeting families outside their homes. While many use this for simply making connections, I think it's possible to get a greater benefit from it.

Brief driveway discipline visits are an excellent way to break the cycle of forcing parents to come to us when we have discipline issues. Call the parents and let them know you are on your way. Tell them you'll meet them in the driveway for a quick chat. If needed, come up with a reason to visit such as dropping off an additional resource from school. Approach the conversation in a positive and helpful attitude to lower parents' defensiveness. Staying in the driveway is many times safer for you and for them. Families can feel judged and insecure about the interiors of their houses, how clean they are, or even their decorations.

Driveway discipline is quick, it's in person, and it helps create positive connections.

Staying in the driveway is faster, too. It lets you get your point across, takes you to them, and is an effective way to bridge that relationship gap. It's more natural too. Standing in a driveway, just talking, can feel much more casual than calling parents into the school's office.

LOVE LIKE A PARENT

Public education in America is a fascinating agreement of trust between parents and schools. Parents don't always realize that when they register their children in our schools, they are handing over responsibility and custody of their children during that time. This duty is serious and comes with many obligations for the safety, education, and overall well-being of our students. The conferring of rights is called in loco parentis, which is Latin for "in place of the parent." It's a concept that took hold in the eighteenth century and has since been legally supported in American schools, granting rights to schools to handle education and discipline in lieu of the parent.

As a parent, no matter what your child does, you know that you will love and take care of them forever. If they get in trouble, even if you are furious, you don't think of sending them away to boarding school forever. (OK, maybe you *think* about it sometimes, but only in fleeting frustration.) The point is that we would criticize parents who wanted to get rid of their kids, but we think exclusion as a means for discipline in school is acceptable, even normal. As parents, we know that we have to figure issues out and keep moving forward, even when our kids do things we don't like. As educators, we should have the same mindset.

Students are people with real problems, real challenges, and real emotions. They go through tough times and make mistakes, sometimes intentionally, but most of the time without thinking. As parents, we understand that kids are kids. They mess up. That is normal. Parents understand kids for what they are and accept the good with the bad; this is something we need to emulate as teachers with our students. When we think of our students as if we were their parents, it helps us to be more caring and patient. The next time you see a challenging student, make efforts to view them through this lens. It will help you as well as them.

REASSURING PARENTS

I once spoke with a parent who was really upset about something that a child did to her child and felt that we (and me specifically) were not taking it seriously. Looking back, I was defensive, and I'm not surprised that this parent went above my head. In fact, in the initial conversation with the parent, I actually told her that she could feel free to call my boss. I even gave her the phone number. So, it went from there about as you would expect. She talked to my boss, obviously upset. To my boss, I looked like I couldn't resolve my own issues. A meeting with me and this parent was scheduled soon thereafter. I was stressed about the whole thing. I felt like I wasn't supported and parents ruled the roost.

At the start of the meeting, the parent asked to record the meeting. My boss was clever in his response. He talked her though the big picture. I've never forgotten his approach. He basically said that our goal was to figure out how we can help her and her child. Recordings make people not speak their mind and put their guards up. Rather than make a recording, it would be better to write a summary of the meeting and take notes. She agreed. Not because she had to, but because she believed that he wanted to help.

During the meeting, we worked through the issue, and I had to concede a few things, mostly that I could have been more supportive of her concern. For years after, I've thought about how poorly I handled that parent's concern, and it has guided my work with parents ever since. Our job is not just to keep kids safe, but to also assure parents and children that we prioritize their safety. Perception matters. It's not enough that we do something. It also matters that people feel something is being done.

And then sometimes, we find that we actually *aren't* doing everything we can. We might feel defensive and even angry that parents call us out on that. Following a set series of compassionate steps completely transformed my work with parents:

- Tell them that you care and prove it with your body language.

- Actively listen and repeat to them what you hear.
- Validate their concerns even if you don't agree with them.
- Tell them you are here to help them and mean it.
- Acknowledge any common ground.
- Be confident and calm, reassuring them things will get better.

It's that easy. Listen. Validate. Support. Investigate. Make a decision. Communicate it. Agree with as much as you can, but don't feel that if you agree with some things, that it means you are agreeing with everything. For example, when parents say their child is being bullied, don't make the mistake I did—automatically questioning it and defining what bullying is for them. All that does is put up their defenses. Just agree. Say that bullying is wrong and you don't stand for it. There, automatically, you found common ground.

Sometimes our actions seem to belie our words. We can tell parents that we are serious about discipline and will do anything to make sure their child is safe, but do our actions substantiate this? To ensure confidence, always call or meet in person if there are concerns about misbehaviors. We created a norm at our school. Good news? Go ahead and email. Bad news? Phone calls are mandatory. Emails don't convey that you care, they only convey that you are trying to make things convenient. When parents call us or email us for help, they are worried, stressed, and looking to you to have a similar level of concern and urgency. Email is good for information and positive news. Email is very, very bad for giving negative news and for showing that you care. If you care, call. No excuses. You may think that a phone call takes more time and is less convenient, but I believe that phone calls not only save time in the long run, they have the ability to completely change the narrative and build relationships even in tough situations.

Be clear about what your plan is and what you do to proactively and reactively address misconduct. Sell it. Provide parents with a general overview and the benefits of your plan. Make sure they know you view their child as a person, not a problem. Don't use pedagogical jargon and don't make things overly complicated or wordy.

It's Not Personal

Not every misbehavior is a personal attack or intentional. My family likes to argue. It's a thing we do. Everyone talks over each other and sees who can win arguments by beating the other into verbal submission. As a kid, I would constantly get into arguments with my peers and with teachers. I never thought of it as disrespectful. I just did it because it was normal to me. I realize now that my teachers probably took it personally and weren't used to a student arguing with them all the time.

What they didn't understand, in part because they didn't ask, was that their normal and my normal weren't the same. Without digging deeper into our students' lives, we won't know the reasons or root causes behind some of the behaviors that may drive us crazy in school. Student norms are not right or wrong. For the most part, they are due to family upbringing, cultural variances, or financial differences. What is normal for one person may be offensive to another, so teachers need to be masters at self-awareness and be more open minded.

We cannot show favoritism to kids that have the same cultural background as us, and we must struggle against any inclination to do so. Being aware of our own and our students' lack of knowledge is the beginning of creating a discipline system based on knowledge of the whole child and the culture they are raised in. We cannot discipline kids for cultural differences that make us feel uncomfortable.

THE NUANCE OF EFFECTIVE PARENT PARTNERSHIPS

Be timely in your response to parents. When parents express concerns, make sure to get back to them quickly. The bigger the problem is, the faster you should respond. Never let it go for more than a day. If you don't respond in a timely manner, they feel you don't care. Parents don't realize how busy you are, and frankly they don't care. You're never too busy to return phone calls to parents. If you can't talk right away, at least send them back an email that says you are aware of the issue or concern and will call them back very soon. It gives you a little more time to investigate or put away other priorities.

Be professional and concise. How you send emails matters. Anything more than a few sentences should be a phone call. I see too many teachers and administrators sending lengthy emails with details or explanations instead of calling. It makes me anxious just reading the emails, I can't imagine what the parents think when they read them. If you have the time to write out that long email, then you have time to call. Another option is to send a quick email expressing that you have a concern and that you will follow up with a call.

Be brave. It's normal to be afraid or hesitant about calling parents. But remember: the more you successfully make these calls, the more natural it will feel. The more natural it feels, the more success you will have.

Think customer service. We must be in a positive and relaxed mindset when we meet and talk with parents. Here's a go-to approach: "Thank you for coming to me and bringing this to my attention. I really appreciate you doing that because it means you trust me to take care of it. How can I help you?" The secret ingredient is that you actually have to mean it.

Keep in mind that every "perfect" kid out there struggles as well. A seemingly ideal household may not be so perfect if there is neglect or even abuse going on behind closed doors. We have to know our students and what they are going through at home. Home life shapes their worldview. Do you need to know the home details of every child you serve? Honestly, probably not. If your students are doing well, learning, and behaving like you are expecting, then you can assume that things are OK. But here is my challenge: If you find yourself in a situation where a child is struggling and you need to take some next steps, get to know the child, their background, and their motivations. Sit down and talk with them. Find out what's going on and what is bothering them. Create trust.

Let parents know that we are all in for them and their children. If a parent says we are not, then it is on us to make them feel different. We put extra stress on ourselves when we get defensive and angry. Parents with concerns are simply part of the job. Having issues doesn't mean that we are failing. Every organization, even the best, has issues. But you can't let those issues consume you. We must we react to the issues and resolve them. Resolving issues quickly also gives us more time to do other things. Just remember that you can't ignore behavioral issues. Learn how to scan your messages and your emails for parents' concerns. Don't let the day go by without addressing these, even if it's the last thing you do for the day.

Set goals for students together with parents. Too many times educators create plans on our own and only later try to involve the parents and show them all the work we have been doing. I've been in meetings where literally I cringed when I realized that we should have brought the parents in from the beginning. How can we expect them to support something they didn't know we were doing? Start with the big picture and think long term. If your goals are too narrow, parents won't buy in because they don't care about the demands that consume our lives as educators. Creating a plan with parents will have lasting benefits for a child's future.

Constantly put money in the relationship bank. Every interaction you have with a family is an opportunity to grow together and prove that you really do care about them and their child. Smile more. Take time to chitchat no matter how busy you are. Make proactive positive phone calls home. Write postcards of encouraging words to send during breaks. Most importantly, be in the moment and intensely focus on them as individuals every chance you get.

PRODUCTIVE MEETINGS

IEP meetings and meetings for discipline can be time consuming, exhausting, and, at times, very stressful. Meetings can be more effective if they are planned out, purposeful, and collaborative.

The struggle strengthens you when it forces you to improve. A contentious situation with one family did just that for me. The family believed that our school was not supporting their child to our fullest, yet our staff felt that we were doing everything we could. I got roped into a meeting by the parents because they felt I would be their advocate—something I feel proud of.

When I get involved, I try to be neutral and listen, but like anything I'm involved in, I'm going to help make it work well. And I can't stand inefficient meetings. I ended up running this meeting, and I took a different approach from the very beginning. I started with a question. Not a discussion of the child's present level of performance or a review of the agenda.

Just a question for the parents: What outcomes do you want for your child?

Then one for the staff: What outcomes do you want for your student?

I asked for big-picture goals, pushing us to think more long term and in a whole-child mindset. So many times, we focus on programmatic nonsense for schooling instead of big-picture skills that will help students in life.

Everyone took a minute to silently write down a statement or two on a piece of paper. One at a time, I asked them to share their statements, and we wrote down comments on chart paper. Each member of the team, no matter their role, was able to have their time and say. Once we got the ideas down, we had a short conversation and then voted on what we thought were the most important of these things. Once we discussed what the group thought the best overall goals were, we started with the more typical IEP meeting.

As you can imagine, the meeting went smoothly after that. We came to a positive consensus on the plan moving forward and all members of the team, including the parents, felt that it was fair and in the best interest of the student.

Building consensus for discipline or IEP meetings at the beginning, not the end, is critical. It sets the tone for open dialogue, listening, and agreeing that we all want what's best for a child. So many times, people just want to be heard and have a voice. So give it to them, but do it in a way that is efficient, fair, and timely. Do it on your terms. Our goal should always be that all stakeholders, teachers, parents, and even students, leave feeling like they were included in the decision and their time was spent wisely.

Here are a few meeting tips:

- Be prepared with materials and an agenda.
- Start and stop on time.
- Have extra drinks and snacks available and even toys for younger children.
- Focus on feelings and active listening. Parents may be coming in very nervous, anxious, or angry. Validate their feelings. Show them that you care. Lower your guard and stop being so defensive. Parents feed off of your energy. When you put your wall up, so do they. When you are anxious, so are they. Relax, breathe, and thank them for bringing these concerns to you.
- Thank everyone. The first thing I always tell parents for discipline issues or special education meetings is thank you: "Thank you for coming to see me and joining me for this tough conversation. That means that you care about your child and that you trust me to help you. I know you want what's best for your child, and so do I. Let's figure this out together."
- Set the stage by explaining the purpose and time frame. Start with the big-picture goals for the child. Use a process. This helps pull the team together from the beginning.
- Agree with parents as much as you can. Using their input is invaluable and creates trust. Knowing your school policies really well helps you know your limits.

- Bring a picture of the student to the next meeting. I often would print out an 8" × 10" picture of the student and put it in a tabletop clear plastic holder for the whole group to see.
- Never go into a meeting without knowing the child. If you have to, go visit the classrooms and catch up with the student, what they need, and how they are doing before the meeting.
- Listen to what parents and students need—sensory-friendly haircuts, a bike, whatever. Don't fight it. Relationships grow from trust and follow-through.
- Consider reframing your meetings when discussing student behavior. Instead of talking about the latest misconduct, flip the meeting on its head and focus solely on celebrating any little thing that is going well. Anything that has worked. Anything that felt like a win.

Education is most successful when we have synergy between families and educators. We can't control what parents do, but we *can* control how we proactively support them, react to their needs, and seek input in our practices. When you embrace families for who they are and what they need, you find that your relationships become strong enough to withstand even the toughest issues.

TIME-OUT

- ➤ What is one fear or struggle you have in working with families? How can you improve in that area?
- ➤ How have you gone out of your way to connect with your students' families and form positive and proactive relationships with them?
- ➤ What are three ways you can improve your meetings with parents?

CHAPTER 10

ENSURE PROGRESS THROUGH FIDELITY AND FOLLOW-THROUGH

WE ALL HAVE DREAMS. BUT IN ORDER TO
MAKE DREAMS COME INTO REALITY, IT
TAKES AN AWFUL LOT OF DETERMINATION,
DEDICATION, SELF-DISCIPLINE, AND
EFFORT.—JESSE OWENS

Like Olympian Jesse Owens in the quote above, NBA legend Kobe
Bryant was a perfect example of the dedication it takes to achieve success. Bryant's level of focus was unparalleled, and the results showed.
He retired with five NBA Championships, was a two-time Finals MVP,
eighteen-time All Star, and a guaranteed Hall of Famer. When Kobe

Bryant tragically passed away, the world mourned and shared stories of his legacy.

Sports trainer Alan Stein Jr. shared such a story about how Bryant's intensity in the game matched the focus he honed working on the basics every day. Stein said he came in one day to observe practice, looking to analyze Bryant's routine and find the secrets to his success. He had to get up early, since Bryant started at 4:00 a.m. with a personal trainer before the rest of his day began. After Stein watched all morning, what he learned disappointed him. The drills Bryant used were the same movements middle school players typically used in their practice. Bryant didn't have innovative or unique practice routines. It was often boring to watch. When Stein later asked Bryant how he could be the best player in the world even though he only used *basic* drills, Kobe simply said, "Why do you think I'm the best player in the world? Because I never ever get bored with the basics."

Anyone who wants to have success must be this dedicated to improving basic skills.

BEGIN WITH THE BASICS

I saved this discussion of fidelity and follow-through for the end because I believe it's one of the most significant *and* difficult ways to improve school disciplinary practices. And instead of sharing an educational story, I wanted to compare the work that greats do in other fields.

Bryant's passion for practice was more than just mere motivation. He lived this as a lifestyle, something he labeled the mamba mentality. Bryant explained this mentality as "focusing on the process and trusting in the hard work when it matters most." He added, "Without studying, preparation and practice, you're leaving the outcome to fate. I don't do fate."[1]

---

1   Chris Schluep interview with Kobe Bryant, "The Mamba Mentality: An Interview with
    Kobe Bryant," Omnivoracious: The Amazon Book Review, October 23, 2018,
    amazonbookreview.com/post/d66e8811-5420-4575-bcee-0a68a747fdc0/
    the-mamba-mentality-an-interview-with-kobe-bryant.

This is a remarkable example of self-efficacy creating new norms of behavior. We may *want* outcomes, but we must *begin* with the basics. The better your basics are, the more effective your work will be. The best don't chase goals. They focus on the work and let the results come to them.

Many of the answers and strategies we need today, such as check-ins, restorative practices, and specific, positive feedback are already in our schools and in our classrooms. Most of these strategies are free or very low cost. In many ways, they are *our* basics. Don't let that fool you into thinking they are easy. The hardest part is staying focused.

Schools are constantly looking to rework their programs, find the quick fix, and implement new strategies. While this may come from good intentions, it often leads to teachers, most of all, feeling the "new program fatigue" seeing years of different administrators and programs come and go without much impact on the students they serve. These changes drain the energy of even our most enthusiastic teachers. Just because we see a really interesting new approach on social media does not mean we have to use it now. Be strategic, not reactionary. Save good ideas on a list and see how, and if, they need to be worked into the overall scheme. It might be a great idea, but we can't keep changing what we are already doing. Different isn't always better. Discipline strategies will only work if we do them *correctly* and *consistently*.

Simplicity and repetition wear down obstacles more than the extravagant. Be more stubborn in your support then the stubbornness we see in students' behaviors. That's one of the most important ways we win in discipline. We outlast them. It's more than just patience. We hang in there longer than they expect or ever thought possible. We. Never. Quit.

BEHAVIORAL SUPPORT PLAN

Every school needs a plan that describes their behavioral instruction and supports they are planning on providing when students have repeated and significant misbehavior. This is not a list of punishments for misconduct. Consequence plans expect failure. Support plans hope for change.

Extra help and interventions need to be identified, agreed upon, and listed out in each tier. The strategies should intensify in both intensity, frequency, and duration as the need increases. For instance, a student with tier-three behaviors is not going to improve with a once- or twice-a-week program. It should happen every day. Educators are first responders, so our sense of urgency should be apparent in our plans as well.

Here is some advice if you would like to create a behavioral support plan: work from what you have in regard to interventions, but start fresh with a new template.

Organize your document into columns with labels for each tier. Tier 1 is generally what everyone receives, and what is "working" to maintain behaviors. Tier 2 is more complicated, which I've come to realize as more of a progression from "concerning" to "challenging," so I've split it up. Tier 3 is where students exhibit very "alarming" behaviors that need intense supports to correct.

In the first row, describe the overall level of concern. This helps to define how frequent or disruptive the behaviors are to the child or school. In the second row, describe the behaviors, or misconduct, you are typically observing in each tier. Finally, in the third row, list out the interventions and supports you plan on providing for students in each tier.

On the following page is an example of a behavioral support plan. You can find the full template for you to use or modify by going to andyjacks.com and clicking on Free Resources.

Tiered Behavioral Support Plan

TIERS	TIER 3 ALARMING	TIER 2 CHALLENGING	TIER 2 CONCERNING	TIER 1 WORKING
OVERALL LEVEL OF CONCERN	IMMINENTLY DANGEROUS, ILLEGAL, AND/OR AGGRESSIVE BEHAVIORS - BEHAVIORS THAT ARE WILLINGLY COMMITTED AND ARE KNOWN TO BE ILLEGAL AND/OR HARMFUL TO SELF, OTHERS, OR PROPERTY.	DISRUPTIVE AND POTENTIALLY HARMFUL BEHAVIORS - BEHAVIORS THAT DISRUPT THE EDUCATIONAL PROCESS AND/OR POTENTIAL HARM OR DANGER TO SELF AND/OR OTHERS	MINIMALLY DISRUPTIVE BEHAVIORS - BEHAVIORS THAT DISRUPT THE EDUCATIONAL PROCESS AND THE ORDERLY OPERATIONS OF THE SCHOOL BUT DO NOT POSE DIRECT DANGER TO SELF OR OTHERS	TYPICAL, INFREQUENT BEHAVIORS FOR AGE LEVEL - BEHAVIORS THAT INFREQUENTLY CAUSE A MINOR DISRUPTION, BUT THE CLASSROOM PROCEDURES, REDIRECTION, AND RETEACHING ARE ENOUGH TO IMPROVE THE MISCONDUCT.
DESCRIPTION OF BEHAVIORS	ASSAULT AGAINST STUDENT OR STAFF; SIGNIFICANT THREAT OF INJURY TO SELF OR OTHERS; SEXUAL HARASSMENT; RACIAL HARASSMENT; RELIGIOUS HARASSMENT; REPEATED BULLYING AGAINST OTHER STUDENT(S); REPEATED ELOPING FROM SCHOOL; POSSESSION OR DISTRIBUTION OF DRUGS OR ALCOHOL; POSSESSION OR USE OF A WEAPON; REPEATED DISRUPTION OF CLASS EVEN AFTER SIGNIFICANT INTERVENTIONS, SUPPORTS, AND PARENT COMMUNICATION	HABITUAL VIOLATION OF SCHOOL RULES OR POLICIES; REPEATED REFUSAL TO COMPLY WITH STAFF DIRECTIONS; ELOPING FROM CLASS OR SCHOOL; REPEATED PHYSICAL AGGRESSION WITHOUT INJURY; REPEATED USE OF PROFANE LANGUAGE; INTENTIONAL TECHNOLOGY MISUSE; BULLYING OF OTHER STUDENT(S); LESS SIGNIFICANT THREAT OF INJURY TO SELF OR OTHERS; REFUSAL TO ATTEND CLASS OR SCHOOL	DIFFICULTY WITH STAYING IN ASSIGNED SEAT AND/OR AREA; MINOR DISRUPTION OF THE LEARNING ENVIRONMENT; PHYSICAL AGGRESSION WITHOUT INJURY; USE OF PROFANE LANGUAGE; SOCIAL CONFLICTS WITH PEERS THAT DISRUPT THE LEARNING ENVIRONMENT; MINOR VIOLATION OF SCHOOL RULES AND POLICIES; MINOR REFUSAL TO COMPLY WITH STAFF DIRECTIONS; REFUSAL TO COMPLETE ASSIGNMENTS	DIFFICULTY WITH STAYING IN ASSIGNED SEAT AND/OR AREA; MINOR AND INFREQUENT NONCOMPLIANCE; BEHAVIORS THAT MAY CAUSE MINOR DISRUPTIONS BUT ARE RELATED TO A KNOWN DISABILITY; DIFFICULTIES WITH SOCIAL SITUATIONS WITH PEERS; INFREQUENT CLASSWORK REFUSAL
INSTRUCTION, INTERVENTIONS & SUPPORTS	FUNCTIONAL BEHAVIOR ASSESSMENT (FBA); BEHAVIOR INTERVENTION PLAN (BIP); DAILY CHECK IN/CHECK OUT CONFERENCES; DAILY SOCIAL SKILLS LESSON; DAILY TAKE TEN CONFERENCES; INDIVIDUALIZED BEHAVIOR MOTIVATIONAL PLAN; MONTHLY PARENT/TEACHER/ADMIN CONFERENCES; IEP BEHAVIOR GOAL & SPED SERVICES TARGETING BEHAVIOR (IF SWD)	INDIVIDUALIZED BEHAVIOR MOTIVATIONAL PLAN; QUARTERLY PARENT/TEACHER/ADMIN CONFERENCES; DAILY CHECK IN/CHECK OUT CONFERENCES; BIWEEKLY SOCIAL SKILLS LESSON; DAILY TAKE TEN CONFERENCES; 2X10 CONFERENCES; INDIVIDUALIZED BEHAVIOR GOAL & SPED SERVICES TARGETING BEHAVIOR (IF SWD)	INDIVIDUALIZED BEHAVIOR MOTIVATIONAL PLAN; QUARTERLY PARENT/TEACHER/ADMIN CONFERENCES; WEEKLY CHECK IN/CHECK OUT CONFERENCES; WEEKLY SOCIAL SKILLS LESSON; 2X10 CONFERENCES; IEP BEHAVIOR GOAL & SPED SERVICES TARGETING BEHAVIOR (IF SWD)	STUDENT INPUT ON CLASSROOM NORMS; CLEAR AND EXPLICITLY TAUGHT DIRECTIONS; RETEACHING DESIRED BEHAVIORS INDIVIDUALLY AND IN SMALL GROUPS; REGULAR PARENT COMMUNICATION

Notice that traditional disciplinary exclusions like suspensions are purposefully omitted from the plan. That isn't what this is about and instead is intended to be instructional in nature. There are many ways that this kind of plan can be structured, but the important things are to be clear on what you will provide when kids inevitably need your help. Be prepared!

FIDELITY

Fidelity means that something is *repeatedly* done the way it is supposed to be done. In the broader sense, fidelity means follow-through and honest accuracy for how we conduct our business. With students who require additional support, or even average students who need regular supports like class meetings, fidelity is an essential component of achievement.

Every day we have an opportunity to do our very best to follow through with the boring parts of our job. It sounds easy, but it's not. We overlook the importance of the boring grind. We take it for granted. We tend to push it off to do something more fun or interesting in the moment. There is a mountain of research that explains why, but we already know we do this. It's natural and normal. But if we want to be great, and help our kids excel, then we need to not be natural. To not be normal. We need to be special.

Let's stop thinking of the boring, daily grind as something that gets in the way of what we really want to do. The boring, daily grind *is* what we should want to do. Those who love the process of improvement are going to be the ones that see positive growth. You cannot get the results without the work. There are no shortcuts in life. There definitely are no quick fixes or easy pathways to helping kids improve their lives. The time spent trying to find them just pulls you further away from what you are trying to accomplish and makes the road that much longer.

Interventions we put in place do what they are meant to do, not what we may want them to do. Each one has a different purpose, and we need to know them inside and out so we can use the right tool for the job. Learn exactly what the designers intended as outcomes. Fidelity matters because for interventions to really work, we must do them the right way and do them consistently. Help everyone get on the same page so that it's crystal clear what the goals are, the duration of time needed, and the frequency of sessions. We all need to do our homework to ensure we know what is expected of us and how to deliver instruction correctly. Nick Saban, head coach of the University of Alabama football team, puts it this way: "Discipline is doing what you're supposed to do, when you are supposed to do it, the way it's supposed to get done."

If we do the program or intervention correctly, consistently, and with passion, we are guaranteed to see progress. If you don't see progress, look first at how you are executing the intervention before changing programs or strategies.

FIDELITY CHECKLISTS

One way to check yourself and your consistency is to create fidelity checklists. These are forms that describe the tasks needed for an intervention to *repeatedly* be done the way it is meant to be done. A fidelity checklist can be simple. List the tasks. Include a place to check them off when they're completed. Add another space for reflective notes on each item.

Many programs have fidelity checks already included, but creating your own has a great side benefit of increasing buy-in and a deeper understanding of the intervention.

An administrator is not the only one that should use these checklists. The best educators I've observed create their own fidelity checks to monitor themselves reflectively. They appreciate feedback, but they are already two steps ahead of any observer doing their evaluation. Fidelity checklists are a way to analyze trends, patterns, and consistency in your own work. Many times, your own analysis will be all you need to find small ways to make improvements. Or, you can have a colleague observe and use a checklist during a planning period or free moment. The more you use them, the more effective and consistent your work will become.

DISCIPLINE IS FREEDOM

Teachers love autonomy and rightly so. Some of the best work educators do is on the spur of the moment, but we can't let the desire for freedom confuse us. We all need discipline, not just our students. Jocko Willink, former Navy SEAL and author of *Discipline Equals Freedom*, explains this well. If you want more time, you need better time management. If you want more control over how your day goes, you need more thought-out planning.

By embracing self-discipline in our work as educators, we can find renewed time and energy to ensure that what we *need* to do *always* gets done. The freedom is felt as a sense of peace when we *know*, not *hope*, that the real work that will make a huge difference is scheduled and organized. Check that box and feel good about yourself. You will end up more relaxed and confident, something you greatly deserve.

Self-discipline and school discipline are not free. They cost energy, time, and dedication. But the return on that investment is immeasurable in the effect it can have on our students.

HABITS TAKE TIME TO CREATE CHANGE

When we're dealing with difficult behaviors on a daily basis and we're frustrated and tired, it's unsurprising that we want these issues to be fixed quickly and for students to make immediate gains. The reality, unfortunately, is much different. Change requires enormous patience. It takes a long time for children and adults to integrate new behaviors into lasting habits.

We get discouraged, disrupted, and, at times, seduced by the false appearance of success after just a short time. That can be especially damaging, because we stop interventions too soon after a string of a few good days. In schools, we need to continue interventions for a long time even after seeing success to help the child sustain new better habits. We want kids to change in minutes, days, or months, and when it doesn't happen, we get frustrated quickly. Kids can't change that fast. The longer the behaviors were ingrained into the child, the longer it takes for the child to break free of them.

We sometimes try to do too many things at once and get stuck not doing any of them very well. We try to pick a new habit that is too big or too much and bite off more than we can chew. We don't change our environment, lifestyle, or supporters, and old habits quickly take back over. We don't have a plan to help us when we falter and fail. We try to do change alone.

We have many students who cause all sorts of discipline issues in younger grade levels, but by the time they graduate, teachers don't even realize they were ever a behavior issue. This doesn't happen automatically just because they aged. It only happened because teachers in each grade along the way worked extremely hard and were focused on improving these behaviors every day. They didn't give up on their kids, and their efforts made a huge impact. Each of these discipline wins gives motivation for us to get right back at it with the next generation of students coming our way.

TIPS FOR SUSTAINING NEW HABITS

Look within and around you to find ways to be more consistent and disciplined.

Missing interventions here and there is like a leak in a boat: even small holes can really cause damage over time. These holes need to be filled in if we want our ship to sail the right way. If we aren't doing the intervention with the frequency that is intended, then how in the world can we expect the intervention to work to change behaviors?

Think of each new intervention as a new habit that we *and* our students need to form *together*. It's important to have clear intentions about what new habit you want, when you are going to do it, and what positive change will result from forming this habit.

Professional learning experiences for educators and administrators should include these kinds of self-improvement skills that are often ironically found *outside* education. *Atomic Habits* by James Clear contains great examples of specific and tangible habit-enhancing takeaways that would greatly benefit us in both life and in our schoolwork. Imagine if we spent as much energy at improving our basic skills as we did in learning new programs? What missed opportunities for growth!

As an educator, you have an advantage. Knowing how people learn and how they form new skills helps us to reflect on how to be more efficient in developing more effective habits. Design your environment so that your habit becomes part of your new norm. Surround yourself with those that support you. Make an overt and public commitment. Focus on the little moments of progress more than only the outcome. Once you start enjoying the habit more than the goal, you are going in the right direction. Become your habit.

DON'T BREAK THE CHAIN

Even highly successful comedians like Jerry Seinfeld have struggled with writing jokes. He struggled with when and how to focus on improving his craft just like so many of us. He realized that if he wrote a joke every day, he would build momentum to keep writing even when times were tough or he didn't feel like it. His idea turned into a technique known as the "Seinfeld strategy" or "don't break the chain." Put a big calendar on the wall and every day you write your joke or practice your new habit, you place a big red X on that day on the calendar. After a few days and weeks, you are proud of the momentum built, and your only new goal is to not break that chain of red Xs.

MONDAY	TUESDAY	WEDNESDAY	THURSDAY	FRIDAY
	1	2	3	4
7	8	9	10	11
14	15	16	17	18
21	22	23	24	25
28	29	30		

With any new skill, frequency beats duration. Spending less time more frequently is always more effective than spending more time less frequently. This is true for learning how to play a guitar, preparing to run a race, or even writing a book. There is something very emotionally powerful about sustaining streaks like this. It reminds us that we don't need to be perfect every day, but we do need do something.

This is why I strongly suggest having interventions done *daily* if possible. It's easier to maintain and sustain daily habits because our body physically and neurologically gets used to the new routine as part of the new norm. It's why you automatically reach for your phone to review social media when you wake up, or you automatically check email when you sit at your computer at work. Our bodies get used to doing what we repeatedly do. When you have interventions scheduled only once or twice a week, it doesn't create the same automaticity. It also doesn't show the same level of urgency to your students, something you may need for misbehavior to really improve.

Use this strategy together with your students. Create a calendar and check the days off together. If you miss a day, don't overly stress about it, but get back on track quickly. Don't let two days go by without the streak starting again. Celebrate each day, each week, and each month that you can keep the new routine going.

JOURNAL YOUR JOURNEY

Another popular strategy in both behavioral and academic settings is to take notes of what you did and what progress you are making. Create a calendar for the week, use a journal, or use a weekly planner. Write your goal for the student at the top as you get into each week. Have a place to write notes on how the session went, if the child met the goal for the day, and things you worked on together.

Add student-performance data to this by creating a rating scale for each day. This ideally can be completed by the students. If their rating is different from what you think it should be, that leads to a great discussion as well. This is not for punishment, so be careful not to admonish the child or they won't be honest in the future. Create a safe place for them to reflect so that they take their responsibility seriously.

Having to do something in writing after the intervention might seem like more work, but these notes are an excellent source of information for identifying patterns that you may not have seen otherwise. They are also a great resource when planning for the next day and skills you want to work on with the student.

WEEKLY GOAL:	Be respectful during interactions with peers throughout the school day	
DAY	**NOTES**	**RATING**
MONDAY	Rough day. He admitted to not being respectful with peers (He said something mean to a friend). We role-played the situation to find better ways to disagree.	*5/10*
TUESDAY	He seemed happier today. He reported no issues with friends.	*8/10*
WEDNESDAY	Great day! He actively went out of his way to help a friend with a math problem.	*10/10*
THURSDAY	Ok day. He reported that he didn't get a lot of sleep last night. Was playing video games late. We discussed the importance of sleep and how it makes us feel when we are well rested.	*7/10*
FRIDAY	Good day. We reviewed the week and any lessons learned. He was very reflective in this one on one conversation. We celebrated!	*8/10*

Teachers can level up this strategy by also asking the students to write their own notes in a journal. This helps the students own the process by using their own words to reflect and rate themselves. If your students don't want to write or have difficulty with writing, have them tell you what to write. They'll start to see their words and ideas on paper. Helping get this done shows that you value their input and reflections.

CREATE A CONSISTENCY CALENDAR

Sometimes it can be difficult to keep up with the overall plan for a student, especially one who needs a lot of different supports. Help yourself by creating a consistency calendar. List all their behavioral interventions in one spreadsheet.

List all the interventions in the first column. Consider adding other items, too, such as class meetings, which can help with improving behaviors. List which staff are responsible for doing each intervention, the days and times the interventions will be implemented, and then a check-off area. In the last column, leave a space to note how many times the intervention was completed that week.

INTERVENTION	STAFF	DAYS	TIMES	MON	TUES	WED	THURS	FRI	SUMMARY
Check-In	Mentor Teacher Mrs. Smith	M-F	7:30 am	X	absent	tardy	X	X	3/5 = 60%
Class Meeting	Homeroom Teacher Mr. Adams	M-F	8:00 am	X	absent	X	X	X	4/5 = 80%
Social Skills Group	School Counselor Ms. Edwards	T, Th	10:00 am	n/a	absent	n/a	Student in office	n/a	0/2 = 0%
2x10	Administrator Mrs. Tanton	M-F	1:15 pm	X	absent	Busy in a meeting	Admin no show	X	2/5 = 40%
Gentleman's Club	School Counselor Ms. Edwards	F	2:05 pm	n/a	n/a	n/a	n/a	X	1/1 = 100%
Check-Out	Mentor Teacher Mrs. Smith	M-F	2:30 pm	X	absent	X	X	X	4/5 = 80%

This also shows you a plan of attack for an issue and helps you reflect on how seriously you are taking this improvement. Students who have a lot of needs should be receiving a lot of help and support. Sometimes you'll realize how much time you are taking the child from class and consider if that really is the best thing to do, especially if it's not working well.

The accountability piece to this is critical if you truly want to be the best for your students. Be clear with how many times the intervention is intended to happen for that week. If an intervention only happens once or twice a week and the student or the staff member involved is absent or has a conflict, then it's easy to see that there will be a big impact on consistency. Sometimes what we think we are doing is giving an intervention, but it may not be actually happening at all once you honestly reflect on what you see in your calendar.

My challenge to administrators is to commit yourself on paper and to the team. If you say you are going to do something, find a way. You can't hold your team accountable if you don't hold yourself accountable first. Leaders lead all the time, not just when it's convenient. And if teachers aren't able to meet with students as much as we would like, then before you start blaming them, instead ask them if there are adjustments you can make to better support them.

There should be no secrets. Students should see the amount of effort going into helping them. Our students need us to be extremely consistent, predictable, and dedicated to the process of improvement as much as anything else.

Just like the great athletes, musicians, or performers, as great educators, we must never get bored with the basics. The basics are what make us great and in turn help our students reach their goals. The basics model consistency for our students. Have pride in staying true to the things you know are effective, and have patience that they will work over time. Be great. Be strong. Cherish this time you have with your students.

TIME-OUT

> What are the biggest obstacles that get in the way of follow-through for your behavioral instruction or interventions? Is it time, energy, too many interventions, not knowing what to do?

> Choose a common instructional tool or intervention that you already use. Create a fidelity checklist using tasks that you feel have the most value in that lesson.

> Try using the diagram below to reflect habits, both for your students and yourself.

> What are two professional habits you would love to break?

> How do these habits interfere with your students' progress?

> What are two professional habits that you would love to replace them with?

> How will those help change things for the better?

Old habits to break:	Results for students:
New habits to start:	**Results for students:**

SCHOOLS SHOULD BE DIFFERENT BASED ON THE STUDENTS THEY SERVE

THERE NEEDS TO BE A LOT MORE EMPHASIS ON WHAT A CHILD CAN DO INSTEAD OF WHAT HE CANNOT DO.—TEMPLE GRANDIN

One of the biggest events that schools do is a promotion or graduation ceremony at the end of the year.

This ceremony is probably typical for many schools, with its speeches, songs, and a packed audience of parents. The highlight of the event is to recognize every student individually on the stage, giving them that special moment just for them. Many times, it gets a little out of control, with kids making fun poses and parents hooting and hollering out of excitement, but that's all part of the fun. We make sure to include every child, and this means that we have to make some adjustments to the program, add ramps, and think through the whole experience to ensure every child and parent can participate.

One year, this inclusive mindset was put to the test. One of our students had a behavioral disability and acted out, sometimes being very disruptive, when dealing with the stress of loud noises or extra stimuli like clapping, yelling, and cheering. The family was going to pull him from the event so as not to add to the stress for their child or the other students. Even the team discussed this as an option. It's a tough call—are we being more supportive by allowing the child not to participate or should we press for inclusion no matter what?

In this case, I decided that I couldn't live with one of our kids not participating just because it was inconvenient to us. Either we are all in for all our kids, or we aren't. Our team moves mountains instead of excluding kids, so we talked it through and came up with a plan.

The main event came up and we had a packed house that day—standing room only with families filling every space available. Everyone was really excited, and the energy was buzzing. Our students sang a special song, and we recognized their participation in various clubs and teams. Students came on stage, posed for pictures, shook our hands, and walked down the aisle for all to see and cheer on. Then it came to this child's turn.

Before he came on, I knew it was my turn to step up. I walked to the middle of the audience, quieted my voice, and made a special request of the audience. I told them of the child's needs and what we needed to do as an audience for him. I asked them to be absolutely silent instead of cheering—no clapping, snapping, cheering, or even waving. We were working on making the moment as sensory-friendly as possible for this student and his day as stress-free as the rest of the students'. This is all about trust and relationships, things I knew we had developed in our school culture, so I quickly turned back to the stage, confident that they would follow directions and go with this plan.

As the young man walked forward with help from a teacher assistant, I stayed completely in the moment and congratulated him on all his hard work at school. I didn't even notice as the room became silent. We had a nice moment together and then I motioned for him to be recognized by his teacher nearby.

Everything was going so smoothly until I began to hear a noise from somewhere in the room. I became quickly annoyed and looked up to the audience to see where it was coming from. I realized that the disruption I was hearing was a soft sobbing sound and it was coming from this young man's mother. She was crying and so overwhelmed at what she was seeing and feeling. Understanding the situation, I knew she never expected her son to be able to participate in these kinds of events. She never felt that her son would have this kind of "normal" experience like other kids. Of course, I started tearing up, and I know most of the crowd did, too.

The moment was special, and I learned an important lesson that day: Sometimes the student doesn't need to learn how to do better in our school. Sometimes our school needs to learn how to do better for the student. When we think of our schools, do we consider how much they should be influenced by the students who we serve? Our kids are different, and if we adjust ourselves accordingly to meet their needs, our schools will be different, too.

The other thing that came to me was the impact that these moments of inclusion have on the rest of the school. I was only really focused on making this adjustment because I felt it was needed for this child, but what I didn't see coming was how much others would be influenced as well. When I looked up with teary eyes, I saw an entire school community affected. Everyone was watching how impactful it was for this family. They felt part of that moment and knew they contributed to it as well. They owned this with pride as they walked out.

I could see and hear this as they left for the evening. One family after the event approached me with a random question. "Dr. Jacks," the mother said, "when you were a child, what did you want to be when you grew up?"

Caught off guard, I replied, "Probably a little bit of everything—lawyer, doctor, police officer..." I still didn't know where they were going with this.

"Whatever you thought, you were wrong," she said. "You were born for *this*."

That finally broke me.

People watch how you support your students, especially those that struggle the most. Your work is defined from *these* moments. It's not perfection people care about, it's effort. You set the tone for your school when you go above and beyond, and it has an exponential effect on your school culture. Don't underestimate the value and think that it's only one child. The work you do for one child is never just for one child. Everything you do sets the tone for the entire school.

TAKE NOTHING FOR GRANTED

A few years later, I attended a funeral for a different student—a former student who had serious medical complications and was supported through another intensive program in our school. I sat in the church quietly, taking it all in and doing my best to be supportive of the family. As the eulogy went on, they described her life's milestones. Again, I was caught off guard when they described her fifth-grade promotion ceremony at *our* school. Even now, it's difficult to describe the emotions that go through your entire core when you hear something like that.

Take nothing for granted. Cherish each moment, the highs and the lows.

The time we have with our students is precious and matters more to them and their families than you realize.

YOU ARE A WINNER

You already have the power to win in discipline. To improve the world around you for your students, your colleagues, and for yourself. You always have.

Stop waiting for the "right moment" to make the changes you think need to be made. Stop asking for permission or looking for others to do the work for you. As Dr. Martin Luther King Jr. said, "The time is always right to do what is right." This isn't a cliché—we owe it to Dr. King and the other giants in the civil rights and inclusive-schools movements to continue their mission. All must really mean all.

Winning discipline must be relationship first. Get rid of the automatic consequences and zero-tolerance mentality. Those archaic practices only feed into the disparity of exclusions and exacerbate their long-term negative impacts. While we may be weighed down in these traditions of exclusion, shame, and blame, we have it within us collectively to shed these practices and ensure our schools focus on progress instead of punishments. We can create a new generation of students who only know a new more positive and productive disciplinary norm. One that is forgiving and supportive. One that teaches students to regulate their emotions and actions. One that considers that we are not just managing classrooms, we are building the foundation of our future, one student at a time.

You may be upset with your current conditions. Or worried about the what-ifs. Take a deep breath. Clear your mind. You are where you are meant to be. Instead of being anxious, get excited. Instead of being frustrated, get focused. Take each issue one at a time. Have confidence that no matter what comes your way, you will take it on and meet the challenge. You can do this!

Your students are counting on you to love them and care for them no matter what they look like, their ethnicity, gender, income, *or* behaviors. They want you to accept them for who they are more than you can possibly imagine.

Society is ready for a new era of school discipline. As educators, we must stop listening to the noise and nonsense and think for ourselves. Our students are crying for help. The behaviors are alarms ringing and calling us to the scene. Are you going to respond to the call? Yes! Are you going to be ready? Yes, you will be! Give everything you have—your heart, your mind, your love. Know what tools you will need so that when you get in the middle of it, you are ready and able! If we want different results, it's time we think, talk, and do different. Go get that discipline win! You got this. *You were born for this.*

ABOUT THE AUTHOR

Dr. Andy Jacks is a highly regarded school leader known for the energy and passion he brings to ensure his students feel valued in school every day. He describes his favorite and most common compliment from visitors to his school as, "It just feels different here."

As an elementary school principal, Andy skyrocketed student achievement and led a cultural transformation that gained local and national recognition for his students and staff, including VDOE Excellence Awards and Distinguished Achievement Awards, PWCS School of Excellence Awards, PWCS Business Partnership of the Year, Virginia Distinguished Purple Star Award, and a school tour by the United States Secretary of Education. Andy has since become principal of a K–8 combined elementary and middle school.

As a senior fellow for the National Association of Elementary School Principals' Centers for Advancing Leadership, Andy works to engage and support school leaders across the country through focused centers on diversity, innovation, the middle level, and women in leadership. He has served on national task forces and has shared at congressional briefings. Andy also serves on the board of directors of the Autism Society of Northern Virginia, where he organizes inclusive and sensory-friendly family events in the region.

Andy has been recognized with, among others, the Virginia Student Training and Refurbishment Best Practice Award and state association awards such as School Bell Award, Professional Development Award, and Virginia Principal of the Year. He is also a Nationally Distinguished Principal.

Andy is a sought-after speaker and trainer, providing professional learning for school districts and associations. He has been featured in publications such as the *Washington Post, Principal Magazine*, and *Education Week*. He resides in Northern Virginia with his wife and three children. Find him online at andyjacks.com.

MORE FROM

DAVE BURGESS
Consulting, Inc.

Since 2012, DBCI has published books that inspire and equip educators to be their best. For more information on our titles or to purchase bulk orders for your school, district, or book study, visit **DaveBurgessConsulting.com/DBCIbooks**.

More from the *Like a PIRATE*™ Series

Teach Like a PIRATE by Dave Burgess

eXPlore Like a PIRATE by Michael Matera

Learn Like a PIRATE by Paul Solarz

Play Like a PIRATE by Quinn Rollins

Run Like a PIRATE by Adam Welcome

Tech Like a PIRATE by Matt Miller

Lead Like a PIRATE™ Series

Lead Like a PIRATE by Shelley Burgess and Beth Houf

Balance Like a PIRATE by Jessica Cabeen, Jessica Johnson, and Sarah Johnson

Lead beyond Your Title by Nili Bartley

Lead with Appreciation by Amber Teamann and Melinda Miller

Lead with Culture by Jay Billy

Lead with Instructional Rounds by Vicki Wilson

Lead with Literacy by Mandy Ellis

Leadership & School Culture

Beyond the Surface of Restorative Practices by Marisol Rerucha

Choosing to See by Pamela Seda and Kyndall Brown

Culturize by Jimmy Casas

Escaping the School Leader's Dunk Tank by Rebecca Coda and Rick Jetter

Fight Song by Kim Bearden

From Teacher to Leader by Starr Sackstein

If the Dance Floor Is Empty, Change the Song by Joe Clark

The Innovator's Mindset by George Couros

It's OK to Say "They" by Christy Whittlesey

Kids Deserve It! by Todd Nesloney and Adam Welcome

Let Them Speak by Rebecca Coda and Rick Jetter

The Limitless School by Abe Hege and Adam Dovico

Live Your Excellence by Jimmy Casas

Next-Level Teaching by Jonathan Alsheimer

The Pepper Effect by Sean Gaillard

Principaled by Kate Barker, Kourtney Ferrua, and Rachael George

The Principled Principal by Jeffrey Zoul and Anthony McConnell

Relentless by Hamish Brewer

The Secret Solution by Todd Whitaker, Sam Miller, and Ryan Donlan

Start. Right. Now. by Todd Whitaker, Jeffrey Zoul, and Jimmy Casas

Stop. Right. Now. by Jimmy Casas and Jeffrey Zoul

Teachers Deserve It by Rae Hughart and Adam Welcome

Teach Your Class Off by CJ Reynolds

They Call Me "Mr. De" by Frank DeAngelis

Thrive through the Five by Jill M. Siler

Unmapped Potential by Julie Hasson and Missy Lennard

When Kids Lead by Todd Nesloney and Adam Dovico

Word Shift by Joy Kirr

Your School Rocks by Ryan McLane and Eric Lowe

Technology & Tools

50 Things to Go Further with Google Classroom by Alice Keeler and Libbi Miller

50 Things You Can Do with Google Classroom by Alice Keeler and Libbi Miller

140 Twitter Tips for Educators by Brad Currie, Billy Krakower, and Scott Rocco

Block Breaker by Brian Aspinall

Building Blocks for Tiny Techies by Jamila "Mia" Leonard

Code Breaker by Brian Aspinall

The Complete EdTech Coach by Katherine Goyette and Adam Juarez

Control Alt Achieve by Eric Curts

The Esports Education Playbook by Chris Aviles, Steve Isaacs, Christine Lion-Bailey, and Jesse Lubinsky

Google Apps for Littles by Christine Pinto and Alice Keeler

Master the Media by Julie Smith

Raising Digital Leaders by Jennifer Casa-Todd

Reality Bytes by Christine Lion-Bailey, Jesse Lubinsky, and Micah Shippee, PhD

Sail the 7 Cs with Microsoft Education by Becky Keene and Kathi Kersznowski

Shake Up Learning by Kasey Bell

Social LEADia by Jennifer Casa-Todd

Stepping Up to Google Classroom by Alice Keeler and Kimberly Mattina

Teaching Math with Google Apps by Alice Keeler and Diana Herrington

Teachingland by Amanda Fox and Mary Ellen Weeks

Teaching with Google Jamboard by Alice Keeler and Kimberly Mattina

Teaching Methods & Materials

All 4s and 5s by Andrew Sharos

Boredom Busters by Katie Powell

The Classroom Chef by John Stevens and Matt Vaudrey

The Collaborative Classroom by Trevor Muir

Copyrighteous by Diana Gill

CREATE by Bethany J. Petty

Ditch That Homework by Matt Miller and Alice Keeler

Ditch That Textbook by Matt Miller

Don't Ditch That Tech by Matt Miller, Nate Ridgway, and Angelia Ridgway

EDrenaline Rush by John Meehan

Educated by Design by Michael Cohen, The Tech Rabbi

The EduProtocol Field Guide by Marlena Hebern and Jon Corippo

The EduProtocol Field Guide: Book 2 by Marlena Hebern and Jon Corippo

The EduProtocol Field Guide: Math Edition by Lisa Nowakowski and Jeremiah Ruesch

Expedition Science by Becky Schnekser

Fully Engaged by Michael Matera and John Meehan

Game On? Brain On! by Lindsay Portnoy, PhD

Guided Math AMPED by Reagan Tunstall

Innovating Play by Jessica LaBar-Twomy and Christine Pinto

Instant Relevance by Denis Sheeran

Keeping the Wonder by Jenna Copper, Ashley Bible, Abby Gross, and Staci Lamb

LAUNCH by John Spencer and A.J. Juliani

Make Learning MAGICAL by Tisha Richmond

Pass the Baton by Kathryn Finch and Theresa Hoover

Project-Based Learning Anywhere by Lori Elliott

Pure Genius by Don Wettrick

The Revolution by Darren Ellwein and Derek McCoy

Shift This! by Joy Kirr

Skyrocket Your Teacher Coaching by Michael Cary Sonbert

Spark Learning by Ramsey Musallam

Sparks in the Dark by Travis Crowder and Todd Nesloney

Table Talk Math by John Stevens

Unpack Your Impact by Naomi O'Brien and LaNesha Tabb

The Wild Card by Hope and Wade King

The Writing on the Classroom Wall by Steve Wyborney

You Are Poetry by Mike Johnston

Inspiration, Professional Growth & Personal Development
Be REAL by Tara Martin

Be the One for Kids by Ryan Sheehy

The Coach ADVenture by Amy Illingworth

Creatively Productive by Lisa Johnson

Educational Eye Exam by Alicia Ray

The EduNinja Mindset by Jennifer Burdis

Empower Our Girls by Lynmara Colón and Adam Welcome

Finding Lifelines by Andrew Grieve and Andrew Sharos

The Four O'Clock Faculty by Rich Czyz

How Much Water Do We Have? by Pete and Kris Nunweiler

P Is for Pirate by Dave and Shelley Burgess

A Passion for Kindness by Tamara Letter

The Path to Serendipity by Allyson Apsey

Sanctuaries by Dan Tricarico

Saving Sycamore by Molly B. Hudgens

The SECRET SAUCE by Rich Czyz

Shattering the Perfect Teacher Myth by Aaron Hogan

Stories from Webb by Todd Nesloney

Talk to Me by Kim Bearden

Teach Better by Chad Ostrowski, Tiffany Ott, Rae Hughart, and Jeff Gargas

Teach Me, Teacher by Jacob Chastain

Teach, Play, Learn! by Adam Peterson

The Teachers of Oz by Herbie Raad and Nathan Lang-Raad

TeamMakers by Laura Robb and Evan Robb

Through the Lens of Serendipity by Allyson Apsey

The Zen Teacher by Dan Tricarico

Children's Books

Beyond Us by Aaron Polansky

Cannonball In by Tara Martin

Dolphins in Trees by Aaron Polansky

I Want to Be a Lot by Ashley Savage

The Princes of Serendip by Allyson Apsey

Ride with Emilio by Richard Nares

The Wild Card Kids by Hope and Wade King

Zom-Be a Design Thinker by Amanda Fox